THE JIGSAW CLASSROOM

THE JIGSAW CLASSROOM

Elliot Aronson
Nancy Blaney
Cookie Stephan
Jev Sikes
Matthew Snapp

A SageView Edition

 SAGE PUBLICATIONS / BEVERLY HILLS / LONDON

For information address:

SAGE Publications, Inc.
275 South Beverly Drive
Beverly Hills, California 90212

SAGE Publications Ltd
28 Banner Street
London EC1Y 8QE

Printed in the United States of America

Library of Congress Cataloging in Publication Data
Main entry under title:

The Jigsaw classroom.

Includes bibliographical references and index.
1. School integration—United States. 2. Elementary school teaching. I. Aronson, Elliot.
LC214.2.J53   372.1'1'02   78-583
ISBN 0-8039-0997-7

FIRST PRINTING

CONTENTS

To "Miss Stark," with fear and affection

Two are better than one, because they have a good reward for their toil. For if they fall, one will lift up his fellow; but woe to him who is alone when he falls and has not another to lift him up. Again, if two lie together, they are warm; but how can one be warm alone?

Ecclesiastes 4:9-12

Preface

We wrote this book in the hope that it would be of interest to anyone who has ever been a student in a public school, who is the parent of a child currently attending a public school, or who anticipates becoming a parent who sends his or her child to a public school. In short, this book is for just about everyone. It describes a way of teaching and learning that not only is enjoyable for teachers and students alike but also increases the academic performance, self-esteem, and morale of school children. Moreover, this method opens the door to warmer, closer friendships within and across racial boundaries.

Too good to be true? Perhaps—but we hasten to add that this method is not the utopian pipe dream of a visionary dreamer. Rather, it is the result of six years of rigorous testing by a research team with diversified training in experimental social psychology, counseling, and school psychology who, collectively, know a great deal about classrooms, teachers, students, school systems, and the research process. After years of testing, this technique has been adopted successfully by school systems across the country.

This book was written as a means of giving our method away to any teacher, school, or school system that wants to use it. Thus while it is true that this book is for just about everyone, it is aimed most directly at the classroom teacher. It not only describes the technique and results of our research procedure, but is also a kind of cookbook, complete with a sample curriculum, classroom exercises, and guidelines for implementation.

It is especially fitting that a body of research on the topic of cooperation could not have gotten off the ground without the active cooperation of a great many dedicated people. Our debt is immense and impossible to repay. Indeed, the number of people who toiled long and hard on this project is so large that, regrettably, we cannot possibly mention everyone by name. To the dozens of elementary school teachers, principals, graduate students, and undergraduate students who worked on this project we offer our sincere appreciation—inadequate as it may be.

There are a few people, however, whose involvement was central and persisted over a long period of time, to whom we want to extend special acknowledgment: Dr. Jack Davidson, Superintendent of the Austin Independent School District, for showing the faith and foresight to open wide the doors of several schools to our endeavors; such gifted teachers and consultants as Camille Tracy, Bebe Nugent, Alice Phillips, Karen Vincent, and Mercene Sherrod; and several particularly hardworking and centrally involved students—Diane Bridgeman, Robert Geffner, Jim Dehoney, John Rozsa, Bill Lucker, David Rosenfield, Tom Grunden, Lindley Robinson, Helen Pankowsky, Suzanne Yates, Barbara Lindsay, Sari Radding, Ruth Tebbets, Ric Bender, Judy Schwartz, Les Kass, Mindy Marantz, Barbara Davenport, Jay Willette, and Martha Morehouse. In addition, thanks are due to Allison Turner for her editorial work and to Faye Gibson, Patti Fox, and Joan Warmbrunn, who typed materials for the project.

Finally, and most importantly, we would like to thank the elementary school students who served as subjects in our research; they proved to be a delightful and refreshingly critical group of colleagues.

This book was completed while the first author was a Fellow at the Center for Advanced Study in the Behavioral Sciences. We wish to express our gratitude to the Center for providing the opportunity, the stimulation, and the facilities which contributed greatly to the project.

A large part of the basic research reported in this volume was supported by grants from the National Science Foundation (NSF) and the National Institute of Mental Health (NIMH) awarded to Elliot Aronson. We are happy to acknowledge that support.

Foreword

Helping our children and youth achieve their full academic potential and become effective citizens is a major goal for educators today. However, the main problems and pressures that are constantly bombarding public education make these goals difficult to attain. Education, family, community, and religion are the four institutions that have major impact on individuals and society. Social scientists have observed that the twentieth century has been marked by a major decline in the effectiveness of three of these institutions: family, community, and religion. There seems to be a movement back to religion in the 1970s, but the family and community are continuing to weaken and have less impact on the development of individuals. In response to these trends, society has increasingly placed on education the burden of solving its problems; at the same time, education is receiving less support from the other three institutions for accomplishing this task.

A primary example of a major social issue which has been left for education to solve is segregation and its many vestiges, which continue to plague America today. In 1954 the Supreme Court, in its landmark decision in *Brown* vs. *The Board of Education, Topeka, Kansas,* seemed very appropriately to suggest that segregated educational facilities are by their very nature discriminatory and for that reason unconstitutional. At that time the justices even went so far as to base their arguments for the majority decision on experimental research data obtained by social scientists that pointed out the negative effect of segregated educational institutions on black Americans. It seemed reasonable, therefore, to require schools to discontinue segregation. But the Court's decision did not effectively take into account the fact that educational technology had not been sufficiently developed to handle the educational problems associated with a history of segregated schools.

There were a number of practical considerations contributing to the difficult problems educators have encountered since 1954. It was difficult to discuss the fact that educators were not prepared to solve a problem that society as a whole had inadequately handled. Anyone who suggested that desegregation was difficult to manage effectively was too often seen as reactionary and bigoted. It seemed that anyone who had the audacity to assert that busing students would not automatically solve the deep-seated social and educational problems resulting from segregated school systems was looked upon with suspicion. Education had many problems, and little research had been conducted in colleges and universities to find solutions. An additional problem for educational administrators was their concern for the economic base of the community from which schools received most of their financial support. The federal government was very cautious about allocating additional funding. Thus we had to develop strategies that would both maintain the financial support available through the white middle-class majority and reverse the injustices of segregation by avoiding "white flight."

For those of us who were firmly committed not only to desegregation but to integration and brotherhood, the problems seemed overwhelming. It was necessary to obtain the full cooperation of administrators, teachers, citizens throughout the community, and any university resources that we could use to help make desegregation work. Experience had taught us that the problems we were facing required serious study, detailed analysis, careful planning, and an extensive commitment of human and financial resources.

In Austin, we had strong faculties and staffs capable of making this type of effort, but additional resources were needed if our efforts were to succeed. At the University of Texas we had a group of professors who were not only well respected for their research and evaluation skills but who also were committed to working for integration. As we were getting ready to unveil our response to the Justice Department, we called some of these people together to discuss the plan. We wanted their ideas and hoped to get their support. In addition, as part of our policy that the school district allow research consistent with our needs and priorities, we informed the professors that we preferred research on techniques which might be used to develop better educational programs in desegregated classes.

Among those from the University with whom we consulted was Dr. Elliot Aronson, who was in the process of designing research studies to examine ways of applying social psychological findings to education. He was especially interested in finding out whether the techniques seen as useful for learning interpersonal skills could enhance achievement and help children "get along better" in school. So a coalition was formed. Elliot and his colleagues at the University brought their research information and skills and we brought our immediate needs for quality education in desegregated schools. Together we sought and obtained a three-year grant to use Title III, ESEA funds to study cooperative teaching strategies. This book documents our joint effort. It certainly does not offer a panacea for all the problems of education or desegregation, but it does describe how cooperation can be both an effective instructional technique and a way of integrating our schools.

We have had an opportunity to see children using the "jigsaw" technique. The amount of work they are involved in, the excitement one feels while observing, and even the achievement test scores attest to its effectiveness. We hope it is a technique that will help other teachers and students. We believe it will be of use for pre-service or in-service for teachers or for the individual teacher looking for ways to improve his or her teaching.

Jack L. Davidson
Superintendent

Kay Killough
Assistant Superintendent
Instructional Services
Austin Independent School District

What We Did and Why We Did It

*I*t is no secret that American public education is in a state of crisis. In 1977 a report by an expert commission headed by Willard Wirtz confirmed what most educators had known (or at least suspected) for some time: during the past several years there has been a large and steady decline in the academic achievement of the average American public school student as measured by the Scholastic Aptitude Test (S.A.T.). Specifically, the S.A.T. scores of high school seniors show an uninterrupted downward trend every year since 1963. Needless to say, this trend has resulted in a growing concern about learning which has produced a demand among a great many parents and teachers for a "return to basics" in education. According to a nationwide Gallup poll conducted in 1977, as many as 87 percent of the sample favored greater emphasis on traditional learning. It is apparent that most parents attribute the decline in student ability to some of the so-called "frills" of educational innovations. That is to say, for a great many people, innovation in the classroom has become synonymous with a lax, laissez-faire atmosphere in which increased attention is placed on the emotional development of children at the expense of basic learning.

There may be some truth to this allegation, but we don't think it is necessarily the case. What's more, our own research has produced solid results demonstrating that there is not necessarily an inverse relationship between the emotional development of the child and her acquisition of traditional knowledge, skills, and abilities in the classroom. Indeed, our research has shown that, under proper conditions, emotional and intellectual growth go hand in hand; proper techniques aimed at increasing a child's emotional well-being also have a positive impact on his learning. What are the proper conditions? On the following pages we will describe an innovative classroom technique that maximizes the performance, the morale, and the well-being of children. The technique is a very simple one that enables children to cooperate with one another to attain their educational objectives in an atmosphere that is exciting and challenging without being threatening or anxiety-producing. In the following chapters we will describe this technique and present the objective scientific evidence for its efficacy. But first, let's take a brief look at the broader issues underlying our concern.

COMPETITION IN SOCIETY

Americans have made a religion out of winning. From the fans in the college football stadium chanting "We're number one" and the little leaguer who bursts into tears when his team loses to Lyndon Johnson who, pouring troops and weapons into Vietnam, declared that he was not going to be the first American president to lose a war, our society asserts its allegiance to victory and its contempt for losers.

What are the consequences of this attitude? How do people behave when competition is a way of life and they are afflicted with this fear of finishing second? They experience a great deal of anxiety when their performance is being observed or measured; they view one another as competitors and potential enemies; they are forever looking over their shoulder lest someone overtake them; and they have difficulty admitting to weakness, vulnerability, or other human attributes. They experience pangs of envy when an acquaintance lands a good job or becomes a successful doctor, lawyer, or barber. And once on this treadmill there is no respite, no resting place. For most people in our society, even reaching great heights of accomplishment does not lead to peace but to still greater anxiety lest they fall from grace. And this anxiety is not unwarranted, as many examples attest. Let us take one incident from the world of sports. In 1975, when Daryl Johnson, the manager of the Boston Red Sox, led his team to a pennant in the American League, he was envied and admired, and after the season ended he was named Manager of the Year—the highest honor a baseball manager can attain. But less than a year later, when his team was having a mediocre season, he was unceremoniously fired. Did he suddenly change from a brilliant strategist to a dunce? Obviously not. He simply committed the one unpardonable sin in this society: he lost. In a society obsessed with winning, each of us is only as good as his most recent performance.

We are not suggesting that competition is evil, or even that it is always dysfunctional. Under many circumstances competition can be fun; it can add zest to an otherwise dull assignment. Moreover, there are situations where a modicum of competition can enhance performance. However, an unrelenting concern with winning can produce very undesirable effects—especially in situations where the stakes are high and where there is little else going on.

COMPETITION IN THE CLASSROOM

Competitiveness is not inborn, but it seems to be so because it is learned so early. Undoubtedly it is communicated and fostered by the family and the media. But one of the major places where it is taught, indirectly but systematically, is the classroom. Before looking at the competitive aspect of classroom education, it might be useful for adults to try to remember what it was like to be in elementary school. Some may recall their elementary school days with feelings of pleasant nostalgia, others with dread and anxiety. Either way, it is almost invariably the teacher who stands at the center of the memory. One of the authors of this volume (E.A.) is rather fond of reminiscing about his elementary school days:

When I recall my elementary school days, it is often with a shiver. Each year there was one person in control of my destiny: she or he had enormous power. Sometimes I loved that person, sometimes I hated her. But almost always I feared her—feared losing her love or incurring her displeasure. My most vivid memory of school is of my second-grade teacher whom I will refer to as "Miss Stark."

Miss Stark, a formidable woman in her late fifties, had many fine and endearing qualities; but among her less endearing qualities was a tendency to engage in overpowering rages. One day in particular stands out in my mind. Miss Stark became incensed at a few of us for "cutting up" and kept the entire class after school. She informed us that we were to write 100 times that we would speak only when spoken to. She told us that each of us could go home only after he had completed that task. She further informed us that she was not to be disturbed for *anything* until we had finished.

When I was about halfway through the task the point on my pencil broke. There I was with an unusable pencil, unable to complete my assignment, terrified of the taskmaster and afraid of asking her if I might sharpen my pencil. What was I to do? I was experiencing a great deal of anguish. After several minutes my anguish turned to panic as, one by one, my classmates finished their task, placed it on Miss Stark's desk, packed up their books, and went home. After several additional moments of intense anxiety, in desperation I tried to gnaw a point on the pencil with my teeth, but it was to no avail. I could not sharpen it effectively enough to write with. Several minutes dragged by. They seemed like hours. I actually began to believe I might never be allowed to leave that classroom. I pictured my mother and father at home, wondering where I was; in my fantasy, several days passed and my parents were in tears. Finally I could bear the anguish no longer, and with all the courage I could muster, I got to my feet and wobbled on rubbery legs to Miss Stark's desk, waited until she looked up from her work, held up my pencil gingerly, and asked in a quavering voice, "May I please sharpen my pencil?" Miss Stark grabbed the pencil out of my hand, scrutinized it suspiciously, glared at me, and said, "Just as I thought! You bit the point off just to have an excuse to disturb me!"

In scores of casual conversations, we've learned that many adults have a "Miss Stark" buried somewhere in memories of their childhood experiences in school. Teachers are only human—the demands of classroom teaching can occasionally try the patience of even the calmest and most placid individuals. Yet our guess is that teachers capable of the kind of harsh behavior depicted above were not in abundance, even in 1939 when the incident occurred. Moreover, systematic observation of a great many classrooms during the past six years leads us to the conclusion that teachers capable of that kind of behavior are rarer still in the 1970s. This change is due to several factors, including the fact that teachers receive better training than they did forty years ago. It is probably also a function of the many innovations that have been instituted by elementary schools in recent years—innovations which have tended to free teachers to relate more fully and more gently with their students. Such innovations as team teaching, programmed learning, and the extensive use of audiovisual aids have added new dimensions to the atmosphere of many modern classrooms. But whether primarily traditional or primarily innovative, virtually all classrooms share two common aspects: the major process that occurs is highly competitive, and the ultimate goal of the competition among students is to win the love and respect of the teacher.

What do we mean by "process"? Whenever two or more people interact, two events occur simultaneously. One of these is the content and the other is the process. Content refers to the substance or subject matter of the encounter; process refers to the dynamics of the encounter, how it occurs. For example, in a classroom the content could be arithmetic, geography, social studies, or music; the process is the manner in which these lessons are taught. It is through the process that people learn a great deal about the world they live in. Indeed, it might even be argued that in the elementary school classroom the process is a broader and more important source of learning than the content itself.

Let us describe the teaching process as it relates to competition. Here is a common scene: the teacher stands in front of the class and asks a question which the children are expected to answer. A few children strain in their seats and wave their hands in the teacher's face, seemingly eager to be called upon. Several other students sit quietly with their eyes averted as if trying to make themselves invisible. When the teacher calls on one of the students you can see looks of disappointment, dismay, and unhappiness on the faces of the eager students. If the student who is called upon comes up with the right answer, the teacher smiles, nods her head, and goes on to the next question. That smile and nod is a great reward. Among the other eager students, however, the success of the fortunate student causes disappointment because now they will have no opportunity to show the teacher how smart and quick they are—until the next question.

Through this process students learn several things. First they learn that there is one and only one expert in the classroom: the teacher. They also learn that there is one and only one correct answer to any question she may ask: the answer the teacher has in her head. The task is to figure out what answer the teacher expects. The students also learn that the payoff comes from pleasing the teacher by showing her how quick, smart, neat, clean, and well behaved they are. If the child does this successfully, she will gain the respect and love of this powerful person. This powerful person may then be kind to the child and tell her parents what a wonderful person the child is.

This process, then, is a very competitive game. Moreover, the stakes are quite high. Most people remember their elementary school teachers more vividly than their high school and college teachers, whose impact was more recent but probably not more profound. As already noted, in elementary school the stakes are higher precisely because the students are competing for the love of one of the two or three most important people in their world. By the time they reach high school or college, the individual teacher has relatively less impact on their day-to-day lives.

If you are a fifth-grader who knows the correct answer and the teacher calls on one of the other students, it is likely that you will sit there hoping and praying that he comes up with the wrong answer so that you will still have a chance to show the teacher how smart you are. Furthermore, those who fail when called upon or who do not even raise their hands and compete have a tendency to resent the kids who succeed. They frequently become envious, and perhaps try to put down a more successful student by branding him "teacher's pet." Or they might resort to physical violence against him in the schoolyard. The successful students, for their part, often hold the unsuccessful students in contempt, considering them to be dumb and uninteresting. The result is that, to a greater or lesser extent, the process which takes place in most elementary school classrooms is virtually guaranteed not to promote friendliness, understanding, and cooperation among the children. Quite the reverse.

DESEGREGATION AND COMPETITION

A few years ago an unsettling and exciting event occurred in the public school system of Austin, Texas. The high schools had been desegregated suddenly by means of a busing program, which contributed to conflict that occasionally flared into violence. As we watched these occurrences we thought of several strategies that might help in the immediate crisis, but we were much more interested in prevention than in cure. Let us explain.

When high school students are at each others' throats, the obvious short-term solution is to slap on a band-aid by, for example, instituting emergency multi-ethnic human relations councils that can begin discussing issues, problems, points of tension, and so forth. While this may be adequate as crisis intervention, it would be far better for society (and far more instructive scientifically) if methods could be devised to *prevent* these tensions from developing. Moreover, it would be far more efficient and effective if these methods could be built in to the structure of the institution rather than stitched on as an afterthought. Specifically, *it would be valuable if the basic process could be changed so that children could learn to like and trust each other not as an extracurricular activity but in the course of learning their reading, writing, and arithmetic.* In order to accomplish this, it would be necessary to deal with students who had not been completely indoctrinated into the existing competitive process and had not yet developed deep-seated distrust for people of different racial and ethnic groups. For this reason, we began doing some observation and research in elementary school classrooms, even though the major crisis was occurring in the high schools.

Before describing our research, a word about the social psychology of desegregation. In 1954 in the landmark case of *Brown* vs. *the Board of Education of Topeka, Kansas,* the Supreme Court declared that separate but equal schools were by nature unequal. This decision was based, in part, upon social psychological research which suggested that sending minority children to separate schools damages their self-esteem. Segregation implies that children from minority groups are inferior; thus there is no way that separate but equal schools can ever be equal, at least in spirit. That is to say, even if schools serving minority children were to have books and teachers and buildings of comparable quality to those serving the children of the establishment, they would be by nature unequal because they are separate, and being separated makes minority children feel inferior.

The Supreme Court decision was not only humane, it was also the beginning of what to us, as working social psychologists, was a very exciting social experiment. In those days, most social scientists believed that, as a direct result of this ruling, prejudice would be markedly decreased because increased contact among children of various racial groups would produce greater liking and understanding. Moreover, we had reason to believe that busing as a means of increasing black-white contact would not only increase mutual understanding but would also provide minority children with a richer educational experience. Indeed, the monumental Coleman Report indicated that the exam performance of black children improved as the percentage of white children in their classroom increased. But Coleman's data were based primarily on black children who were living in neighborhoods that were predominantly white and who were not, therefore, typical black children. For example, one might suspect that their parents, since they had chosen to live in white neighborhoods, might differ in many significant respects from the parents of children living in the ghetto.

And, sure enough, recent data by Harold Gerard and Norman Miller show that when busing is used to integrate schools, no such improvement in the performance of black children occurs. Very recently, Walter Stephan undertook a careful, thorough review of the dozens of studies of desegregation extant at that time. He found no clear evidence that desegregation increases self-esteem among minority students. Rather, in 25 percent of the studies the self-esteem of minorities *decreased*. This is ironic and tragic when viewed in the context of the reasoning behind the 1954 decision.

The crucial variable seems to be not busing itself, but *what happens* when the kids get off the bus—that is, the process that exists in the typical classroom. And, as we have indicated, the academic competitiveness that exists in the classroom is one that does not encourage a student to look benevolently and happily upon his classmates; it is not a process that is designed to increase understanding and interpersonal attraction even among people of the same racial or ethnic background. Rather, the process induces competitiveness, one-upmanship, jealousy, and suspicion. When one adds to this situation the already existing racial tensions that are present in any urban society, it is little wonder that violence may often result.

Moreover, the situation is even more volatile than we have pictured it. When schools are massively desegregated in most American cities, students are competing with each other on unequal ground. Specifically, in most communities the ghetto is not known for its superior educational facilities; existing conditions can completely frustrate even the most gifted teacher. Consequently, just prior to busing, the knowledge, reading skills, intellectual curiosity, and ability to compete in cognitive skills of most minority-group members is probably inferior to that of their white counterparts. Thus the typical black or Chicano student entering the new classroom finds herself in a highly competitive situation where she is virtually guaranteed to lose. Is it any wonder that minority children in newly desegregated schools experience an increase in anxiety and a decrease in self-esteem?

Needless to say, we no longer believe that desegregation, in and of itself, is a panacea. We now believe that it is a necessary first step toward helping children like and respect one another as individuals, and that changes in the classroom process itself are vitally important.

Returning now to the Austin project, if our understanding of the process was correct, it was necessary to find a way to change the process—that is, to change the atmosphere in the classroom so that the children would no longer be competing against each other but would begin to treat each other as resources. Further, if our reasoning was correct, changing the process could have a beneficial effect upon the interpersonal relations of all of the students, not simply minority-group members. Recall that in the process we described, there was only one human resource in the classroom: the teacher. The teacher is the source of all answers and virtually all reinforcements. In that process there is no payoff for consulting and collaborating with one's classmates. They are your enemies, your competitors; they, too, are trying to impress the teacher and get that love and respect that you want. Indeed, if a student does try to use the other kids as resources in the typical classroom, he may be reprimanded. Thus not only is the process highly competitive and destructive to interpersonal relations—which is itself a heavy cost—but, in addition, a potentially valuable pool of human resources in the classroom is not fully utilized.

THE COOPERATIVE CLASSROOM[1]

Our attempt to change the process was a relatively simple one employing a synthesis of principles gleaned from our years of work on small-group dynamics and social interaction. First, we changed the basic structure of one expert and thirty listeners by placing the students in small groups of about six students each. We changed the role of the teacher so that she was no longer the major resource for each of the learning groups *by creating a process that made it imperative that the children treat each other as resources.* This was achieved in two ways: (1) we structured the learning process so that individual competitiveness was incompatible with success, and (2) we made certain that success could occur only after cooperative behavior among the students in a group. In a traditional classroom, the students are often rewarded when they succeed in attracting the teacher's attention by outshining their competitors. In the cooperative classroom, the students achieved success as a consequence of paying attention to their peers, asking good questions, helping each other, teaching each other, and helping each other teach.

How did this come about? An example will clarify. In our initial experiment, we entered a fifth-grade classroom where the students were studying biographies of great Americans. The upcoming lesson happened to be a biography of Joseph Pulitzer. We created a biography of Joseph Pulitzer that consisted of six paragraphs. The first paragraph was about Pulitzer's ancestors and how they came to this country; the second described his childhood and growing-up years; the third covered Pulitzer as a young man, his education, and his early employment; the fourth told of his middle-age years and how he founded his newspaper; and so forth. Each major aspect of Pulitzer's life was contained in a separate paragraph.

We mimeographed our biography, cut it into six one-paragraph sections, and gave each child in the six-person learning group one of the paragraphs. Thus each learning group had within it the entire biography of Joseph Pulitzer, but each child had no more than one-sixth of the story. In order to learn about Pulitzer, the students had to master their paragraph and teach it to the others in their group. For example, David was responsible for Pulitzer as a young man, Marianne for Pulitzer as a child, and so forth. Each student took his paragraph, read it over a few times, and then joined his counterparts from the other groups. That is, David, who had Pulitzer as a young man, consulted with Bonnie, Ted, Jane, and Carl, who had also been given Pulitzer as a young man. They could use each other to rehearse and to be sure they understood the important aspects of that phase of Pulitzer's life.

A short time later the children went back to their groups, where they were informed that they had a certain amount of time to teach that knowledge to each other. They were also told that at the end of that time (or soon thereafter) each person would be tested on his knowledge of Pulitzer's *entire* life. Clearly the students had to depend on one another to learn all their material. The process is highly reminiscent of a jigsaw puzzle, with each student possessing a single vital piece of the big picture. Because of this resemblance, we came to refer to our system as the "jigsaw" model.

When left to their own resources in such a structured situation, the children eventually learned to teach and to listen to each other. The children began to learn two important lessons: (1) none of them could do well without the aid of every other person in that group, and (2) each member had a unique and essential contribution to make. Suppose you and I are in the same group. You have been dealt Joseph Pulitzer as a young man; I have Pulitzer as an old man. The only way that I can learn about Pulitzer as a young man is if I pay close attention to what you are saying. You are a very important resource for me. The teacher is no longer the sole resource; indeed, he is not even in the group. Instead, every kid in the circle becomes important to me. I do well if I pay attention to other kids; I do poorly if I don't. It's a whole new ball game.

A jigsaw classroom is not a loose, "anything goes" situation. It is highly structured. Interdependence is required. *It is the element of "required" interdependence among students which makes this a unique learning method, and it is this interdependence that encourages the students to take an active part in their learning.* In becoming a teacher of sorts, each student becomes a valuable resource for the others. Learning from each other gradually diminishes the need to try to out-perform each other, because one student's learning enhances the performance of the other students instead of inhibiting it, as is usually the case in most competitive, teacher-oriented classrooms. Within this cooperative paradigm the teacher learns to be a facilitating resource person, and shares in the learning and teaching process with the students instead of being the sole resource. Rather than lecturing to the students, the teacher facilitates their mutual learning, in that each student is required to be an active participant and to be responsible for what he learns.

Cooperative behavior does not happen all at once. It typically requires several days for the children to use this technique effectively because it is very difficult to break old habits. The Austin children had grown accustomed to competing during their first four years in school, and for the first several days the students tried to compete, even though competitiveness was now useless. Let us illustrate with an actual example, which is quite typical of the way the children stumbled toward the learning of the cooperative process.

In one of our groups there was a Chicano whom we will call Carlos. Carlos was not very articulate in English because it was his second language. He had learned over the years to keep quiet in class because, frequently, when he had spoken up he had been ridiculed by some of his classmates. In this instance he had a great deal of trouble communicating his paragraph to the other students, and was very uncomfortable about it. He liked the traditional way better. This is not surprising, because in the system we had introduced Carlos was forced to speak, whereas before he could avoid discomfort simply by remaining quiet. The situation is even more complex. It might even be said that the teacher and Carlos had entered into a conspiracy. Carlos was perfectly willing to be quiet. The teacher had learned not to call on him because when she did he would stumble, stammer, and fall into an embarrassed silence, and some of the other children would make fun of him. Her decision probably came from the kindest of intentions—she did not want to humiliate him; but by ignoring him, she had written him off, which reinforced his counterproductive behavior. In addition, the teacher's attitude implied that Carlos was not worth bothering with—at least the other children in the classroom almost certainly received that message. They believed that there was one good reason why the teacher was not calling on Carlos: he wasn't smart. Indeed, it is likely that even Carlos began to draw this conclusion.

Let us go back to our six-person group. Carlos had to report on Joseph Pulitzer's middle years, and was having a very hard time. He stammered, hesitated, and fidgeted. The other children were not very helpful; they had grown accustomed to a competitive process and responded out of this old, overlearned habit. They knew what to do when a kid stumbled—especially a kid whom they believed to be stupid. They ridiculed him, put him down, teased him. During our study kids said such things as "Aw, you don't know it," "You're dumb," and "You don't know what you're doing."

In our first study, the groups were being loosely monitored by a research assistant who was moving from group to group. Observing this situation, our assistant intervened by saying something like: "O.K., you can do that if you want to; it might be fun for you, but it's *not* going to help you learn about Joseph Pulitzer's middle years, and you will be having an exam on Pulitzer's life." Notice how the reinforcement contingencies have shifted. No longer do the children gain much from putting Carlos down, and they stand to lose a great deal. After a few days and several similar experiences, it began to dawn on the children that the *only* way that they could learn about Pulitzer's middle years was by paying attention to what Carlos had to say.

Out of necessity they gradually began to develop into pretty good interviewers. If Carlos was having a little trouble communicating what he knew, instead of ignoring him or ridiculing him, they began to ask probing questions. They became junior versions of Dick Cavett, asking the kinds of questions that made it easier for Carlos to communicate what he was thinking. Carlos began to respond to this treatment by becoming more relaxed, and as he relaxed his ability to communicate improved. After a couple of weeks, the other children realized that Carlos was not dumb, as they had originally thought, and began to like him. Carlos began to enjoy school more and began to see the Anglo kids in his group not as tormentors but as helpful and responsive.

BASIC RESULTS

What happened in Carlos' group is a good example of the technique and how it frequently worked to produce beneficial effects, but it hardly constitutes acceptable scientific data. For that, we must turn to our field experiments in which we systematically investigated the effects of the jigsaw techniques on interpersonal attraction, self-esteem, and happiness in school. We instituted the jigsaw technique in several classrooms for six weeks and assessed its effectiveness by taking measures at the beginning and end of the period—comparing the performance of the children in the jigsaw classrooms with the performance of children in more competitive classrooms being taught by effective teachers.

Our findings are quite consistent:

(1) Children in the jigsaw cooperation classrooms grew to like their groupmates even more than they liked others in their classroom.

(2) Both Anglo and black children in the jigsaw classrooms started to like school better (or hate school less) than the Anglo and black children in competitive classrooms.

(3) The self-esteem of the children in the jigsaw classrooms increased to a greater extent than that of children in competitive classrooms.

(4) In terms of the mastery of classroom material, children in the jig-

saw classrooms performed as well or better than children in competitive classrooms; specifically, while Anglo children performed as well in either type of classroom, black and Chicano children in desegregated schools performed significantly better in jigsaw classrooms than in competitive classrooms.

(5) Children in the jigsaw classrooms cooperated more and saw their classmates as learning resources more often than children in competitive classrooms did.

These results have been replicated and extended in other school systems. (A more thorough treatment of this research is presented in Chapter 7.)

While the jigsaw technique was developed as an attempt to bridge the gap between children from different ethnic groups, our results make clear that its function is not limited to multiracial situations. The technique curbs some of the undesirable aspects of excessive competition and increases the excitement children find in cooperating with one another. Thus our research has demonstrated that what seemed to be a deeply ingrained kind of behavior—competitiveness—can be modified. Our aim is not to eliminate a child's ability to compete; a certain amount of competition can be fun and may, in many circumstances, enhance performance without producing negative consequences. What we want to do is *teach cooperativeness as a skill* so that when a person finds herself in a situation where cooperativeness is the most productive strategy she will not view everyone in sight as competitors and doggedly try to defeat them. Also, the jigsaw method can be a useful addition to individualized learning programs. When individualized instruction utilizes independent study it frequently results in reducing the child's opportunity to develop social skills in the learning environment. Complementing individualized instruction and other classroom experiences with jigsaw groups could provide a beneficial balance as well as an interesting set of experiences. In this context, it should be noted that the children in our experiments were exposed to the jigsaw technique for only a small fraction of their time in school—often as little as three or four hours per week. The rest of the time they were learning in a generally competitive atmosphere. Our results show that children can learn the skills of cooperation and that cooperative activities can have an important and beneficial effect on their lives, even when these activities are presented in a basically competitive atmosphere. This is encouraging because it means that parents and teachers do not need to choose between cooperation and competition; both can occur in the same classroom. Moreover, by working in jigsaw groups, the children learned that *it is possible to work together in a helpful way without sacrificing excellence* and that working together increases their self-esteem and happiness in school. Finally, it is our contention that experiencing cooperativeness will increase tolerance for temporary failure both in others and in oneself; our hope is that this technique can lead to a reduction in the anxiety that is too frequently associated with performance in our society.

In the following chapters we will discuss in greater detail what happens in a jigsaw classroom as well as how to set one up. We will also provide a more precise account of the procedure and results of our research.

NOTE

1. Throughout, we use the term "cooperative classroom" or "jigsaw classroom." By this we do not mean to imply that cooperation is used exclusively in the classroom, merely that it is systematically used some of the time.

Turning a Collection of Individuals into a Cooperative Group

2

*T*he typical classroom contains a crowd of different personalities. Each one is shaped by different family and
cultural environments and comes with his or her own needs,
skills, attitudes, and techniques of surviving—if not excelling—in
the competitive world of school. A teacher in a jigsaw classroom
will find this diversity an advantage. But before this technique
can function constructively the students must acquire the ability
to work with their classmates in a cooperative, supportive manner. This cooperativeness is the crux of the jigsaw approach, yet
it is a skill which seldom has been cultivated extensively in
school settings. For that reason, spending some time to develop
that cooperativeness is an important first step of the jigsaw
method. There are definite techniques for developing cooperativeness and the term we use to cover them is *teambuilding.*

THE IMPORTANCE OF TEAMBUILDING

At the beginning of the year, it is too much to expect students with little preparation to know how to work together
cooperatively on a difficult academic task. It is asking them to
learn both the content and a new process at the same time, and
probably neither will be mastered. The resulting frustration will
just cause discouragement and boredom. Instead, teachers have

found that jigsaw classes are more successful when students have a chance to work together through teambuilding exercises *before* the curriculum material is tackled in the jigsaw format. This serves to make the process familiar and comfortable before any content learning has to begin. A short period each day for one or two weeks is generally sufficient time for this teambuilding, and it is well worth it in the long run.

Although teambuilding exercises may be conducted with the class as a whole, they usually are done in small groups so the students can experience the organization of their new learning environment from the beginning. To develop group cohesiveness, we usually assign students to their first jigsaw group and do the teambuilding within that group. Before we discuss the specifics of teambuilding, though, let's look at the composition of a typical jigsaw group and the rationale behind it.

GROUP COMPOSITION

The size of a jigsaw group may vary from three to seven children, with five or six an ideal size. The fewer the children in a group, the more limited their opportunity to learn how to work with a variety of people. On the other hand, in groups larger than six or seven, individual students do not seem to have enough chances to speak, and consequently their interest drops.

Jigsaw teachers have found a diverse group of students is more desirable than a homogeneous one. Thus jigsaw groups should ideally contain both boys and girls, assertive and non-assertive students, fast and slow readers, and members of different racial or ethnic groups. Such diversity in the jigsaw group extends the potential learning resources available to each student. For example, the slow learner may be stimulated and helped by a more highly motivated student who is, in John Holt's phrase, "a competence model within reach." The slow learner in turn provides the quicker student with a valuable opportunity to acquire effective tutoring skills. Furthermore, exposure in jigsaw groups to children with different personalities and backgrounds is enriching in a way that can extend beyond the classroom. A jigsaw student is challenged to develop empathy and tolerance, and must learn to work effectively toward common goals with persons differing from himself in experience and capability. Increasingly, this latter skill is one that is needed in most occupations in the adult world, where there is a frequent demand for flexibility and the ability to work constructively with others in a task group.

We might say here that the "diversity is best" rule has its exceptions. For example, if the topic is math and if much of the learning is sequential, some teachers have chosen to form homogeneous groups of the advanced students, while they themselves use more traditional methods with the remainder of the class. Also, placing best friends and worst enemies in the same group might provide a desired diversity of skills, but such combinations are best kept out of the same groups, at least in the beginning. Best friends tend to form a coalition, a sort of competing group within the group; and the unresolved but powerful feelings of enemies obviously distract from the process goal of learning to cooperate. After students have some practice with the jigsaw method, existing personal relationships might not need to be an important consideration in composing groups. Indeed, a teacher may even decide that students who dislike each other, having learned some tolerance in other jigsaw groups, could now profit from being in the same group.

In some sense, every jigsaw group is an experiment based on the teacher's knowledge and intuition of what the students need and are capable of at any given point in their development. The duration of a group is also flexible. For example, at the start of a year, students may need to work together in the same group five or six weeks. Later, when their group skills have evolved more fully and they can adapt more readily to others, the teacher may want to change the groups every few weeks so that students have a chance to work with a greater variety of people.

TEAMBUILDING AND HELPING SKILLS

Imagine that you are a teacher and your students are in small jigsaw groups for the first time. The more assertive children are excited and fidgety, ready for a new opportunity to prove themselves. Those children who tend to be shy may already be withdrawing under the pressure of changed circumstances. Your teambuilding goal is to give all the children the experience of being valuable group members. Moreover, you want them to discover that for some tasks, a giving, attentive, cooperative strategy is more effective than a competitive one with each person working individually to beat the others. You want them to see that, for these tasks, competitive behavior both hinders the group and makes individual success impossible. Here is a teambuilding exercise you might use, called the Broken Squares Game.

All group members receive six pieces of a puzzle. They are told that the object of the game is for each person to end up with a completed square. The pieces each person needs are distributed among his teammates, so he is not going to be able to complete his puzzle alone. Nor can he simply take a piece he needs from someone else. He can only give away one of his own pieces to help another group member complete his or her square. To encourage each person to be actively helpful to others instead of waiting to see who can help him, no communication is allowed. This means a participant cannot ask or signal for someone to pass him a piece. For each member of the group to end up with a completed square, *all other* members must take the initiative. They must see what pieces others require and reach over to give those pieces to them. In other words, the emphasis is on giving and cooperating.

Now, switch places and imagine for a moment you are a student. How would you feel? In all probability, you'd feel happier and happier as the other group members noticed what pieces you needed and as you were able to reciprocate. In this way cooperative behavior is reinforced in emotional and practical terms. There is clearly no reward for trying to be better, faster, smarter than everyone else. The issue changes from "How can I come out on top?" to "How can we help each other so that we may all do a better job?" Teamwork is promoted by the realization that the success of each depends on the success of all.

At the end of the game, students in each group are given time to discuss how they completed the squares, what feelings they experienced, and what frustrations, if any, developed. This discussion itself is an important teambuilding activity. The students are looking not only at how they reacted as separate individuals, but also at their group process—how their group as a whole worked. Learning to evaluate their group process is an important part of the jigsaw method because this is how students come to take responsibility for their own behavior. We will discuss this in more detail later in the chapter, but first let us turn to another preliminary teambuilding activity, the development of listening skills.

LISTENING SKILLS

Many students, particularly those from more typical classrooms, may have developed a habit of not listening to their fellow classmates. Picture this situation: the teacher first calls on Christopher, who gives the wrong answer. He then calls on Julie, who is eagerly waving her hand. *She gives the same wrong answer.* How can this be? Doesn't she realize that that answer is wrong? Actually, as most experienced teachers are well aware, this is not an uncommon occurrence. It happens because the student is watching her teacher for cues, signs of approval or disapproval that indicate whether the question is still available to be answered. In other words, Julie is simply not listening to Christopher. The importance of listening to a fellow student may never have occurred to her, not even as part of the strategy to win approval for herself, and certainly not as a means of learning something about the material under question. In a jigsaw classroom, however, if the students are not listening attentively to each other they are not going to be able to learn what the other students are trying to teach. Moreover, listening to the others is the *only* way to learn the material.

Clearly it is advisable for the teacher to provide an opportunity for the students to work on developing listening skills before curriculum material is approached. For example, in one exercise teachers have found both useful and popular, two students interview each other: Who are you? Where do you live? What did you eat for breakfast? What do you like or dislike most about school? Then, on the basis of that information, each student introduces his partner to another pair of students, who in turn make their introductions.

There is a further reason to impress upon students the importance of listening to each other. If the speaker in a group senses that she is not being listened to with interest or appreciation, she is likely to feel rejected and to lose the motivation and commitment to do well at teaching. For example, if Michele is intently drawing horses during Sara's presentation, Justin is folding paper airplanes, and two others are passing notes, Sara is clearly without an audience. Of course she won't want to continue teaching. And the next time her turn comes up, Sara is not likely to be enthusiastic about preparing her material.

It is vital that steps be taken to prevent such a process of discouragement from getting started. That's the reason listening skills are an important part of the teambuilding. In a more general sense, the preliminary teambuilding sessions can help students begin to learn what to do when a problem arises that makes the group experience less than satisfying. It is essential that the students eventually come to understand that whether the group process is satisfying or unsatisfying is really within their control. That is, each group member is somewhat responsible for the manner in which the group is functioning.

DEVELOPING A COOPERATIVE LEARNING ENVIRONMENT

Few students have a very clear idea of what is involved in cooperative and constructive group behavior. They have some notion that it is usually disruptive to shout or punch each other, but they usually don't know which positive actions promote a good group atmosphere. Jigsaw teachers have found it wise to set aside teambuilding time for students to answer the question "How should we behave to help the group work more effectively?" A useful technique to initiate this discussion is to "brainstorm." Brainstorming is a method of eliciting many ideas in a short period of time by rapidly recording all the suggestions without permitting any discussion or evaluation of them. For example, I might ask a group of students what supplies we would take along on a trip to Mars. The answers would come thick and fast. Some would be sensible and practical, like oxygen, food, space suits, and so forth. Others might present some problems, like toilet paper (how could we get it inside our space suits?). Still others would be totally whimsical, like a waterbed. The point of brainstorming is to encourage the spontaneous expression of ideas without evaluation, criticism, or discussion.

Following the brainstorming, the suggestions can be arranged according to priority. Thus, if the groups were working on the above question of making their group process more effective, each group of students might take five minutes to list twenty or thirty positive behaviors. The final list could then be posted in the classroom for all to see. A point worth emphasizing is that it is more useful for these behaviors to be stated positively than negatively. A student learns more by thinking about what he ought to be doing, such as "listening while another member is talking," than he does by thinking about what he ought not to be doing, such as "not talking while someone else is speaking." The negative statement fails to lead him to positive behaviors that can be reinforced. It only tells him what not to do, and what might be punished.

The more specific these behavioral prescriptions, the better. For example, if the students decide they should "show each other they are listening," the teacher might suggest they list the ways they are able to know that someone is listening to them. The students might list such behaviors as:

(1) Looking directly at the speaker.

(2) Nodding that you understand her.

(3) Rephrasing what she has just said.

(4) Summarizing her statements.

(5) Reflecting the feeling behind his statements. (For example, when Jaime says, "I don't think we'll ever finish at this rate," Diane might reflect, "It sounds like you're discouraged by our getting off the subject.")

(6) Letting the speaker know that you have heard by building on her ideas. (For example, "Besides what you've said, I think . . . .")

(7) Leaning toward the speaker while listening.

(8) Smiling with reassurance.

What happens in such a brainstorming session is very significant: the students begin to think in terms of group process.
But more important, it is the opening wedge in developing
individual responsibility, when students begin to realize that
they themselves are able to develop a cooperative learning
environment. Should a problem later arise in a jigsaw group,
the students have specific standards by which to recognize it,
diagnose it, and cope with it constructively. They will be able
to try, effectively, to change the group process to make it more
rewarding. The old familiar tactics of blaming someone, calling
names, whining, or simply withdrawing will need to be used
much less frequently.

This skill of evaluating the group process is an important
element of the jigsaw method. During teambuilding exercises
the students often are asked to focus on such questions as:
Are we sticking to the task? Are we encouraging everyone to
participate? Are we listening to each other attentively? Are we
treating each other with kindness and respect?

Once the students begin an academic unit, group-process
evaluation is facilitated by using group-process cards which each
student fills out during the last five or ten minutes of the group
session.

It is important that the students actually write their im-
pressions of the group rather than just think about them. Our
experience shows that formally writing down an evaluation
increases a student's motivation to examine the group process
and to commit himself to improving it. We have also found that
it is helpful to have each student write his or her individual
opinion first and then join the others in filling out a group card.
In this way each student has something specific in hand to share
with the others. Without the chance to write their opinions
first, students will often merely say that everything is "okay" or
"not bad," and let it go at that. The problem with this is twofold: first, they're not exploring in depth the ways they might
improve their group and, second, they're missing the chance to
focus on the ways they're already doing a good job. In this last

instance, they miss the rewards of seeing how well they are functioning and their positive behavior is not specifically reinforced. (See Appendix C for a sample group-process report.)

INTERGROUP COMPETITION

So far in this chapter we have been emphasizing cooperation in the classroom. At the same time, we should point out that there may still be a place for competition during the early transition phases, if that competition occurs between groups and not within groups. Many teachers have found that when jigsaw groups are first established, group identity and group motivation are weak. If such is the case, a small amount of intergroup competition may stimulate children to become a "team," to help each other with greater enthusiasm so that their group can accomplish more than the other groups. However, while using the well-practiced skills of competition to develop cooperative skills may be effective, it is a tricky business: the already established system has considerably more vigor through familiarity than the new, and can easily take over. It would be well for teachers who use intergroup competition to have the students discuss the possible negative effects of such competition and the positive effects of intergroup cooperation. Eventually, it is advantageous for the various groups to begin cooperating. To facilitate this, the teacher might set up tasks in such a way that they could be more easily accomplished if the groups shared their work. Or perhaps a bonus of some sort could be given if all the groups did well.

MOTIVATION CHANGE: A LOOK AHEAD

After two weeks of teambuilding activities, students will find they have some power to control group process by solving the problems which inevitably arise as they learn to work together. Because of this, working together gradually becomes an increasingly pleasurable and productive experience. Now they are ready to face a new task, that of using the jigsaw method to teach each other an academic subject.

An interesting change soon becomes apparent in what motivates a student to learn academic material. Previously, as is well known, student drive was based on the desire to be the best in relation to other students, not to do one's best. In competitive classes a student might work very hard, but not necessarily for the joy of learning as much as she could. Instead, the motivation more often is the pleasure of attaining a comparative advantage over the other students in grades, in the esteem of the teacher, and so forth. Although anxiety-provoking, this competitive environment can be exciting for the successful students. Unfortunately, for the slower students who are not "winners," who cannot beat the others in academic performance, it all too often leads to discouragement and lowered motivation.

However, as students carry what they have learned from teambuilding sessions into jigsaw groups, the motivation to out-perform others becomes tempered. It is replaced by a sense of responsibility to the group, by the desire to help others and to share ideas. Importantly, this desire does not dampen performance—it improves it. Children find that the joy of discovery can be enhanced when shared with others. When learning occurs in a low-anxiety atmosphere of mutual acceptance, it becomes more rewarding; it is, simply, more fun. Teachers often find additional changes occurring in their classrooms. One of our teachers, during the third week of using the jigsaw, wrote:

> It is exciting to see that Michele and Teri, two outstanding students, now seem to be more challenged by helping the slow students than by trying to impress me and the other students with how smart they are. In fact, their cooperativeness has transferred to non-jigsaw modes of learning. For example, recently Michele sensed that Bill was having trouble with his division problems. Without hesitation, she quietly pulled up a chair and began to help him. Bill was able to accept her help appreciatively. As other students in the class began to notice how well Bill was doing in math, they came over to Michele for help. Now Michele gives help to anyone who needs it, and so does Teri.

Again, it would be naive to expect this kind of behavior to occur early in the process. Indeed, at the beginning of the group some of the students might express some frustration at the change of atmosphere. It is vital for the teacher, in jigsaw learning, to help these students adapt to their new role as "teacher-learner" rather than as competitor.

Special Roles in the Classroom: 3
Teacher and Group Leader

*T*here are two roles in the jigsaw classroom which merit special consideration: that of teacher and of student group leader. These two are closely related. The role of the group leader is patterned after the teacher's role; they are both "facilitators," a term we use for persons whose function is to lead a group, help the members look at how they are working together, and examine how they can improve their interaction in order to accomplish some task. Ideally, the ultimate goal with jigsaw groups is to reach a point where a facilitator is no longer necessary because group-process skills will have been taken over by the members. In the jigsaw classroom, the teacher, as facilitator, seeks to help the children teach themselves in smoothly functioning small groups. In any given classroom there may be five or six groups and, since he cannot be everywhere at once, each group has a leader, a teacher's "assistant" through whom group-process skills are passed to each student, and who also acts as an organizer for the business of the day. The role of group leader need not be a permanent one. The group members may take turns being the leader.

THE TEACHER'S ROLE AS FACILITATOR

To understand techniques that student leaders will be learning and practicing, let us begin by observing the jigsaw teacher (their model) at work. He is moving about the classroom from group to group, checking how each group is progressing on its task, keeping eyes and ears open for any problems that may be developing. One of the students calls out to him in exasperation, "Mr. Johnson, Nicolas won't listen." It is *not* the responsibility of Mr. Johnson to solve the problem with an order such as "Nicolas, get to work immediately," although this might be the case in a more traditional setting. Instead, he might ask the group leader what the students themselves have done to solve the problem. For example, he might ask if the group is doing everything it can to help Nicolas understand the material. In this way, he is reminding the students of their responsibility to help one another learn. The leader might then ask Nicolas if he is listening and, if not, what's the source of the problem. Nicolas may not be listening because the events of the Boston Tea Party are being presented too rapidly for him to follow. In such a case, the teacher might suggest to the leader that she ask one of the quicker students, "Since you know the facts now, would you review them for all of us?" On the other hand, Nicolas might be bright enough, but merely bored by the way the material is being presented. Perhaps Scott is simply reading it off a card in a halting monotone. The teacher sees that Scott has not really mastered his material, so he may call the leader aside and suggest that she try to get Scott to put the material into his own words or relate it to something in his own life that the others could understand and relate to as well. In this case, Mr. Johnson would be helping all the children understand how to approach and penetrate any new material.

Finally, there may be times when the teacher judges it necessary to set aside the academic material altogether. A quick review of something the students discussed during earlier team-building sessions may be in order. For example, he might respond to the complaint about Nicolas by asking the students to focus on group process: "What steps might be taken here to encourage full participation?" The group, when given the opportunity, can usually come up with a creative and effective solution for its own problems, a solution that is often better than one the teacher suggests.

It is important to emphasize here that, from the beginning,

the teacher should make interventions through the student group leader whenever possible. This will establish and validate the leader's facilitating role for the other students. Also, by-passing the leader will undermine the leader's commitment to help, which in the long run would mean more work for the teacher since the students would continue to depend on him as chief problem solver. Thus the teacher may phrase his interventions as requests or suggestions to the leader: "Perhaps you should check to see if everybody understands those facts now" or "You might tell the group that calling Nicolas names is not going to help them learn the material." Questions asked, suggestions made, the very words used tend to be picked up by the group leaders. This modeling speeds the development of effective groups under student guidance.

In addition to acting as a consultant-facilitator for the various groups, the teacher is also an information resource. As such, he makes available interesting academic materials. Then when a student asks a question on subject matter, the teacher can answer with another question: "Where could you look that up?" Again, the intent is to guide every student toward greater independence. And, to guide toward interdependence: "Brooke, could you show Larry how to use that reference book you were using yesterday?"

Giving up their traditional authority is understandably difficult for some teachers. However, for most it is exciting to watch the responsibility for learning shift to the students. To create the proper atmosphere and setting for learning becomes a matter of student responsibility. No longer can they blame the teacher for a boring class or a dull discussion. If the classroom environment is not a rewarding one for them, they know they can and should do something about it. The power and skill are theirs.

Even so, it is obvious that the teacher is not abdicating all authority; he is not simply turning the students loose to find out in a hit-or-miss fashion what works. Behind the scenes the teacher designs a structure, a step-by-step procedure to help the students learn how to make use of each other effectively. In each classroom there should always be firm boundaries within which the groups function. The alert teacher carefully notes the pace at which the students can successfully take charge, and then works within those boundaries. Let's look more closely at how the teacher facilitates the development of effective group leaders.

THE GROUP LEADER

During teambuilding sessions the teacher may wish to stress the usefulness of a group leader. He can do so by having the children focus on specific ways a leader should function in order to be effective. You will remember that teachers generally have group members brainstorm a list of their own tasks and responsibilities, followed by a discussion which organizes and evaluates these ideas. The same technique could be employed with respect to the group leader. The following sample list will give some idea of the role of group leader.

(1) Helps the group get organized.
 (a) Gets folder.[1]
 (b) Appoints a timekeeper and recorder to take notes on the day's events.
 (c) Convenes and adjourns the group.
 (d) Helps the group discuss the process of how they interact.
 (e) Helps set the agenda.

(2) Keeps the group on the task by reminding them of the task, by asking the recorder to read what has been accomplished, by asking the timekeeper how much time is remaining, and so forth.

(3) Serves as liaison between teacher and group.
 (a) Understands and/or clarifies assignments with teacher before trying to describe them to group.
 (b) Shows enthusiasm for task, and does not say, "This is what we have to do today because the teacher said so."

(4) Models productive member behavior.

(5) Asks questions for information and/or clarification, never just to show off.

(6) Is patient and understanding; shows belief that the team can be effective if it follows certain rules of working together.

(7) Politely asks members to do things.

(8) Helps the group deal with disagreements by staying impartial and helping members to understand each other rather than finding blame. (For example, asks members: "What's bothering you?" "Can you be more specific?" "How can you help things go better?" "Is this what you mean?")

(9) Encourages feedback as to how he can be more helpful by asking, for example, "How can I do it better next time?"

Although each group composes its own list, the lists are usually remarkably similar. Composing this list permits the students in each group to have some influence on how its future leader will act. In a sense, the group is giving its leader permission to follow the list. However, it should be clear that having a leader does not relieve the members of their own responsibilities. For this reason many teachers post the previously developed ideas for member behavior beside those for leader behavior, for ready reference once the jigsaw groups begin.

Since teachers need help they can count on when first establishing the jigsaw process, they usually select the group leaders themselves, choosing reliable students who can handle extra responsibility. Such students may, in fact, thrive on the extra challenge; it can function to keep their interest in school alive. Later on, however, leadership can rotate among the members of each group.

Group leaders do require some special training. At first the teacher may simply meet with them informally, perhaps over lunch, to explain the jigsaw process and to discuss their role. Then as the jigsaw experience gets underway, such meetings can be held once or twice a week to give the leaders continuing support and an opportunity to share problems and solutions. We will suggest here, however, a training process somewhat more structured than a casual lunch-hour discussion. Our observation, supported by teacher experience, indicates that this training is well worth setting aside special time for. This is particularly true in the beginning, when all the students are unfamiliar with jigsaw group experience.

There are essentially two parts to this training process for the group leaders. First, there are discussions on some aspect of how to lead a jigsaw group; second, there is role-playing of difficult group situations. For example, in the first lesson for student leaders, the teacher might begin by conducting a ten-minute discussion on leader behavior. At the end of this discussion she asks the students to review the way she led them, noting those behaviors of hers which helped the group and those which hindered it. Since this is the first lesson, and since she is the teacher, her request might meet with a sudden and total silence. In this case she would find it necessary to probe. For example, "Do you remember when Josh and Donna were talking at the same time? Do you remember what I said, how we solved that problem?" Probably she did little to hinder the discussion, but she may not have been perfect and so might offer this observation: "I think perhaps I wasn't fair to Jim. I wanted to finish quickly and so I interrupted him too soon. How else could I have acted without hurting someone's feelings and yet still gotten the group to finish its work?"

By exposing herself to criticism, the teacher, a traditional authority figure, is setting an important example. A leader, whether teacher or student, is still part of the group. He or she can always benefit from having constructive behavior praised and mistakes pointed out tactfully. The goal is to have an effective group in which each student can learn, and it is essential for the leader to help the group reach that goal. Training sessions, then, include a discussion of some issue, followed by a critique of the quality of leadership displayed during that discussion.

The second aspect of leadership training involves role-playing. The teacher asks the leaders to brainstorm problem situations they might encounter. The resulting list would include such issues as what to do when:

(1) Certain members never talk.

(2) Someone dominates the discussion.

(3) Members call each other names.

(4) Certain members will not work.

(5) Someone wants to work alone.

(6) Everyone talks at the same time.

Next they choose the three most commonly raised issues and talk briefly about ways to handle them. The group then role-plays each of the three situations. After each role-play, the student who played the leader receives feedback from others on what he did that was effective in dealing with the problem and what other things he might have tried. During this critique, the teacher encourages them to discuss the costs and benefits of each possible leader behavior. At this point, it is helpful to role-play the same situation again and compare the results with the first attempt. Then the group can summarize the general leadership behaviors that are effective in each situation.

Let us summarize this process:

(1) The students list problem situations with which they will be concerned.

(2) They role-play the situations.

(3) They critique what has just occurred.

(4) They role-play again.

(5) They develop general principles for intervening.

We have found this to be an extremely effective training procedure. The first step, wherein the students generate their own list, increases their motivation to learn ways to deal with those situations. Any technique which involves students in setting their own goals for what should be learned raises their commitment to reach those goals.

The second step, role-playing, accomplishes two things. Most importantly, it permits students to experience beforehand various situations in an enjoyable way. They have a chance to practice new leadership behaviors and to become accustomed to leading difficult groups. Of almost equal importance, role-playing develops empathy; that is, the students experience what it feels like to be the type of student whose role they are playing. For example, if one student plays a shy, withdrawn group member who is being pushed to participate, he may actually begin to experience the fear and resentment that a shy student might feel when being pressured. Learning this can aid group leaders in being more sensitive to a variety of students and, hence, more helpful.

The third step, a critique of the role-playing, is an exciting way to encourage the students to develop their skills for analyzing group dynamics. Because they have just experienced the situation, each member is an expert on how the other members' behavior affected his own feelings and responses. When students share the way they felt about each other during the role-playing, they increase their awareness of how different behaviors cause various reactions. For example, Susan might say, "When you ordered me to be quiet, I got mad because you were so bossy and I wanted to quit this group." Because they were just "playing a role" and were not really very emotionally involved, they can discuss what happened more openly and without too much need to explain or defend what they did. This also helps them become more comfortable giving and receiving feedback, an important skill for a group leader to develop.

The fourth step, a repeat of the role-play, helps the student to learn and practice the modifications suggested by the group. The final step of developing the general principles for intervening as a leader flows directly from the critiquing done in the third step. As the students talk about how they felt and acted when the leader said one thing and how they might have behaved if he had said another, they begin to see that each behavior has certain potential benefits and potential costs. For example, they might role-play what to do if two students were joking and laughing rather than working. The leader might intervene by saying, "We need to complete this task, and you two need to help. Sit up and pay attention." When critiquing, it would become clear that firm direction like this might work with, and even be needed by, some students but might only create resistance and resentment among others. In addition, even if it were effective in getting members to work (a benefit), it might cause them to become dependent on the leader to solve all their problems (a cost). A less directive approach—for example, "How can we encourage each person to do his work?" —might get the group to solve the problem itself (a benefit), but might take fifteen minutes and result in some frustration over the failure to get further on the assigned task (a cost).

From discussions like these, the leaders will develop an awareness that there are few ways to behave in a group that are totally "right" or totally "wrong," but that some ways may be more appropriate than others in certain situations. After weighing the costs and benefits in different situations, they will slowly develop their own general principles to guide their decisions. For example, they will learn that the more authoritarian and directive they are, the faster work will get accomplished at the beginning. However, at some point giving orders will foster dependency and apathy, followed by resentment and resistance. Discussing these group issues gives the students an increasing awareness of how to be effective discussion leaders.

This then is the leadership-training procedure most teachers who are experienced in the jigsaw method would recommend. It takes time, perhaps two or three thirty- to forty-minute sessions a week for the first couple of weeks, and thereafter once every three weeks or so until the leaders change. When new group leaders are selected later in the year, they will need far less training because they will have participated in jigsaw groups and learned from the leaders of their groups. The question is: what are all the other children doing while the teacher is involved with the leaders? If there is a teacher aide available, or another teacher who is also setting up a jigsaw classroom, the two can share responsibilities. In the preliminary teambuilding days the other teacher or aide could be overseeing teambuilding exercises with the rest of the class. Thereafter, while the leaders are training, other students could perhaps be at work developing curriculum materials. For example, they could be drawing or cutting out pictures to supplement the lessons they will attempt to teach their teammates. The daily life of a typical classroom, as any teacher knows, necessitates intricate scheduling. The time and energy devoted to leader training, however, will be worth it, even if it means slightly more planning and more work, because the result will be effective leaders helping their groups work productively and with enjoyment.

The training of leaders is not simply the learning of a limited practical skill by a select group of students. Indeed, the entire endeavor can be regarded as a unit teaching the behavior of small groups. Such experiential learning can be invaluable in helping students to gain insight into effective and ineffective processes in any problem-solving group, from congressional committees and city council meetings to their own families planning a vacation. Moreover, since leadership in jigsaw groups rotates, virtually all of the students will have the opportunity to benefit from this unique learning situation.

NOTE

1. The folder generally contains the group-process cards and a summary of the work done to date.

What a Jigsaw
Classroom looks like 4

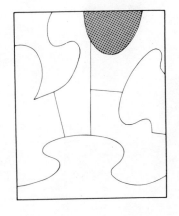

*I*n preceding chapters, except for an occasional example to illustrate a point, we have not offered a complete picture of a jigsaw class at work. There has been more tell than show. Now we would like to describe what a one-hour visit to a sixth-grade classroom might show, using Ms. Taylor's class as an example. Ms. Taylor is an exceptional teacher who has been using the jigsaw approach for two years; her class is a model one. As with every successful enterprise, to develop a smoothly functioning jigsaw classroom requires hard work and experience. In their early stages few classrooms proceed as well as Ms. Taylor's. But her class is not an ideal version of how a jigsaw classroom *might* function; rather it is an accurate picture of how a very good jigsaw class *does* function.

Ms. Taylor welcomed us into her class and informed us that the students were about to begin an hour of social studies. They had been assigned to new groupings a week earlier when they began a new unit on the colonial period. We learned that, as in many classes, students functioned at varied reading levels. For example, three or four were reading at only the first- or second-grade level. As was the case in other classes in this school, even children with severe learning problems were maintained in regular classes. Ms. Taylor told us that this class had been using the jigsaw approach for three months and that the students had learned to work together very well. She also said that the students were accustomed to having observers and our presence would not disturb them.

Ms. Taylor then rang a bell and when the students were quiet, she introduced us. She asked the students to get into their groups and to spend five minutes reviewing before outlining the agenda for this period. For each six-person group, the member whose turn it was to be the recorder got the group's folder from the box. In the group nearest us, Kevin, the recorder, returned with his folder; Lisa, the team leader, asked him to read the brief notes that described where they had stopped the previous day. Then she asked, "What are we going to do today?" and the group developed the hour's agenda. When that was accomplished, Lisa asked Kevin to read the previous day's notes on how the group had functioned. Scanning the group-process evaluation cards, Kevin commented that the group needed to improve its ability to stay on the task and not get sidetracked. He also cautioned the group that it appeared they were falling behind and would not be ready to be tested on the material they had agreed to study. With an impatient look at Amy, who was not listening, Kevin concluded by saying that Amy had agreed to pay attention. Amy looked a little embarrassed and annoyed, but did not change her behavior; that is, she continued to look inattentive for the next ten minutes, at which time Lisa reminded her to listen.

On this particular day, Ms. Taylor rang her bell after the first ten minutes in order to allow each group to get a sense of what the other groups were doing. Each group was asked to describe its academic goals and tell what materials it had already finished. Each group leader asked someone from his group to report. For example, Ms. Taylor called on Lisa, who nodded to Jon. Jon reported that they had finished studying the economic conditions in the colonial period and had given the material to another group along with suggestions on how to use it. Today they were going to start studying colonial religions, having just received the materials from another group. We noted that even though at any one time the groups may have been working on different topics, they seemed quite willing to help each other.

For the colonial unit Ms. Taylor had prepared jigsaw activity cards for each particular topic.[1] Lisa passed a card to each person: Mark, Kevin, Amy, Nicole, Jon, and herself. The cards suggested ways that each student could help focus discussion on important issues and directed the student to additional resource information, such as reference books and, for the students who had difficulty reading, tapes. Performance objectives accompanied the material to help the student know specifically what must be presented. For example, the student teaching about Puritanism found on the card, "Each member of your team should be able to name two colonies in which Puritanism was found." Since each student was responsible for teaching different information, each knew that the others were relying on him for his part. If each group member did not teach his or her individual part well, the group as a whole would not be able to meet its performance objectives. The group members realized that in order to help each member teach well, they needed to listen carefully and ask good questions.

Ms. Taylor had mimeographed the resource material that accompanied each card so that the students could promptly begin work on their presentations. Since Amy was the fastest worker, she helped Jon, who was having difficulty with some of the words on his sheets.[2] After ten minutes Lisa interrupted to see how much more time they would need; they decided to begin discussion in five minutes. The students continued reading over their material, jotting down notes on essential points they wanted to teach the group, and thinking of ways to raise the discussion questions suggested on the activity cards.

After the five minutes had passed, Lisa called the group back together. They decided to try limiting themselves to ten or fifteen minutes on each topic in order to finish the following day. Nicole's presentation was to be the first piece in their jigsaw puzzle of information. Her topic was "religious persecution" and she began by asking her groupmates to close their eyes, as was suggested on the activity card. She told them to imagine they deeply believed in a religion, yet the police would not let them go to their church. They were told to try to experience such things as living in England three centuries ago . . . being beaten and put in jail . . . suffering economic losses . . . their children being taught another religion at school . . . deciding to leave . . . sorrow at leaving . . . the tough, perilous trip across the ocean . . . a difficult start . . . hardships, but also schools where their children learned their own religion . . . living, by choice, with people who shared their beliefs, and so on. Although Jon and Amy seemed to have trouble paying attention, the fantasy appeared to help the others prepare for the discussion. Nicole asked them to open their eyes, and began to tell them about the persecution in Europe and why many people gave up so much to come settle a new land. She read some questions from the activity card: "If these people gave up so much to be able to practice their own religion and to have it taught at school, do you think they would want to let other religious views be taught in their schools? If they believed dancing was bad, do you think they would pass laws against dancing? If they believed everyone should go to their church, do you think they would pass laws to make people go? After all, they had given up a lot to live in just the way they wanted." Most of the students nodded yes. Then she read the next question, "But what if you and a friend didn't believe in Puritanism? Should you have to learn that at school, or have to go to a Puritan church?"

A lively discussion ensued, covering the topics suggested by the questions on the activity card. We were very impressed to see the amount of understanding the students had of what it was actually like for settlers such as the Puritans, of what issues they had faced and how they actually had dealt with them.

The students were so involved in the discussion that Lisa needed to interrupt in order to remind them of their time limits. The group quickly reached consensus to extend their allotted time and resumed the discussion. Jon became rather excited and told Lisa she was "stupid" for saying that she thought that the Puritans ought to be able to force everyone to go to their church. Lisa quickly retaliated by saying that Jon was too "dumb" and "weird" to know anything about religion. At this point Amy interrupted and said, "Wait a minute! You know we're not supposed to call names. Stick to the topic. Anyway, Ms. Taylor said there were no right or wrong answers, so quit acting like know-it-alls." Even though Amy herself was calling people names, the group did get back on the subject. They decided to move on to the next topic after a brief discussion of the final question: "In our group, do we ever persecute each other or force our beliefs on each other, as happened to the colonists? Why might that happen here?"

Although most of our attention as observers had been focused on the students, we also were noticing some interesting things about Ms. Taylor's behavior toward the groups. She was moving from group to group, checking the quality of discussion and behavior. Sometimes she merely listened to a group. More often she knelt beside the leader to ask a question or make a suggestion. In particular, when she came to our group she quietly mentioned to Lisa, the leader, that it did not look as if everyone were participating. (In fact, we had observed that Mark had said nothing and that his chair was pulled back slightly outside the circle.) Ms. Taylor asked Lisa what the group might do to help create an atmosphere where everybody would feel able to participate. After Ms. Taylor left we noted that Lisa interrupted by saying, "Let's wait a second. Are we helping everyone to say whatever they're thinking?"

Kevin responded sharply, "Mark's been off in the clouds again. Why don't you talk like everyone else?"

Amy said, "Quit picking on him. If you weren't talking all the time, maybe he could say something!"

Lisa interrupted to help Mark and the other group members figure out how to make it easier for Mark to share his ideas. They decided to pause briefly between people's comments to make sure that others would have a chance to add their own ideas. They also encouraged Mark to say whatever he wanted, and Lisa and Jon told him that whenever he *had* talked in the past, they had liked his ideas.

The group we were observing was in the middle of a second lesson when Ms. Taylor interrupted the class to announce the end of the group session. She asked them to jot down how far they had gotten on their agenda and then to spend the last five minutes with their group-process cards. Each person filled out his own card, using several criteria to evaluate how he worked in the group that day. Lisa then asked the group as a whole to rate itself in several categories and, using these ratings, they discussed how they could work more effectively the following day.

ANALYSIS

While this was a rather typical sample of a good, experienced jigsaw group at work, the behavior of the children was far from perfect group behavior. Amy, for example, was inattentive, perhaps bored. While we cannot be certain after only a brief observation, we would guess that her inattentiveness might be attributable to the fact that things were moving too slowly for her. If this were the reason, the group leader or the teacher would want to focus on this problem. One solution would be to get Amy involved as a teacher of the slower students in her group. The goal would be to change her perception of her role from bored student for whom things are going too slowly to active helper. Then Amy's inattentiveness should decrease and her excitement increase.

While Kevin noticed Amy's inattentiveness, his mild annoyance was communicated rather punitively. As Lisa becomes more familiar with her leadership role, under the tutelage of Ms. Taylor, she will learn to handle such a situation more productively. Similarly, as she becomes more adept, she will be able to bring quieter students like Mark into the discussion in a tactful way before his inactivity becomes a source of embarrassment to him. Moreover, Kevin will probably learn to express his feelings without attacking others.

How will he learn? And how could the squabbling and namecalling which occurred in this group be reduced? One advantage of the small group is that it occasionally allows the focus to be on the squabble itself, which can be a means of helping children learn more about interpersonal relations—that is, about how to communicate with one another more effectively and less disruptively. The next chapter discusses such a learning process.

NOTES

1. If the teacher had not prepared these materials, we might have seen the group leader dividing up the tasks among the members (e.g., one religion for each student to research), and then the members would go to such available resource materials as social studies texts.

2. If all the groups in the class had been working on the same material, we would probably have seen one representative from each group form temporary counterpart groups for fifteen minutes, during which each subgroup would cover a different topic. The representatives would help each other prepare to teach this material, so that when they went back to their own groups they could do a good job of presentation. See the next chapter for a more detailed discussion of the use of counterpart groups.

Squabbling: The Need for Communication Skills 5

*T*easing, feuding, putting each other down, these activities, unfortunately, are as much a part of life in the classroom as reading and math, occurring in virtually all classrooms in all sections of the country. The jigsaw group is an intimate situation, one where the children work in very close association and depend heavily on each other. Because of this, conflict may seem more frequent, particularly at first, than in a competitive classroom.

In a jigsaw classroom, the children are not individually isolated units. They are not forced by the arrangement of the classroom to curtail their conflicts and postpone them until recess. Moreover, any group (such as the one described in the previous chapter) has certain built-in conflicts attributable to the age of the children. Among eleven- and twelve-year-olds, for instance, feelings of attraction and annoyance tend to run strong, especially between children of different sex. Yet as the year progresses, a certain ambivalence may appear. A boy and a girl may regard each other with familiar suspicion, but a degree of interest may also begin to emerge. One day they may show exaggerated horror at finding they must sit together, the next they may seem to enjoy working together, or vice versa.

Besides these complexities, there are the conflicts which arise around the task itself. A certain amount of material must be covered by tomorrow, but someone is holding back the group.

Someone else is pushing ahead too rapidly and leaving the others behind in confusion. In most competitive classrooms there is very little that teachers can do except ignore the conflict, reprimand the offenders, or deliver a lecture on how important it is to get along with one another.

Because the jigsaw group tends to bring conflicts to the surface, it provides the setting and the tools for the children to work through those conflicts and learn something about themselves and one another in the process. Moreover, because only a few children are involved, the rest of the class need not be interrupted in its work. Accordingly, the teacher may decide to use an instance of petty quarreling as a vehicle to help the children learn about how their behavior affects others.

To demonstrate how the teacher might do this, we will use a simple, unsubtle instance of negative communication: name-calling. But first, let's look closer at this phenomenon. As we all know, name-calling is a great American cultural tradition. It's now incarnate in the television character of Archie Bunker, who calls his son-in-law Meathead and his wife Dingbat; indeed, he has a put-down name for just about everyone. Since the show began, Dingbat and Meathead have passed into the vocabulary of a generation of TV viewers. They are funny names; it's fun to tease a brother or sister with them. Let us suppose Jason is a boy who, like most children, watches television an average of five hours a day. In almost every show, whether a police show, cartoon, or comedy, somebody gets called a name by somebody else. It may be for laughs, but Jason comes to know that name-calling is what you do when you feel superior to a person, or at least when you want to look that way. Life seems to mirror television: when Jason's older sister stays out too late, their father disgustedly calls her boyfriend a hippie. And when his mother opens the latest medical bill, she mutters that the doctor is a crook. Jason comes to know that name-calling is what you do to express displeasure.

What Jason does not know is that name-calling, while revealing feelings of disgust or displeasure, also masks or hides a whole complex of other feelings. If expressed they would place the name-caller in a vulnerable position—the worst place to be in a competitive society where, as explained in Stephen Potter's book *Gamesmanship,* there are two positions: one-up and one-down. An insult places you one-up. In our example, Jason's father may be afraid to see his daughter growing up. Does that make him old? Maybe he is jealous because until recently she was his little girl. Now he is being replaced, so he puts down her boyfriend. If he admitted to feeling anxious or jealous, it would make him vulnerable. In the world of one-up and one-down this would be risky. And what about Jason's mother? The doctor's fee may or may not be outrageous. The point is that she feels the need to put the doctor down as a crook, needs to feel morally superior at least, because she felt dehumanized on the examination table, a fool when he said there was nothing wrong with her, and now he is demanding all that money.

With such experience behind him, Jason goes to school and settles down in his jigsaw group to complete some work for the test tomorrow. But alas, Sara has her Civil War battles all mixed up. "You dingbat," Jason says, somewhat mildly. "I am not, you creep," Sara replies heatedly, and task is forgotten; the squabble is on.

What is going on here? What kind of intervention is needed? It may help to look at this brief interaction as a chain of events.

Jason has some feelings and, at least in part, he expresses them. Sara perceives that his verbal behavior is directed against her, and it arouses certain feelings in her, feelings which Jason may have had no intention of arousing. It is natural for Sara, in her hurt and anger, to interpret Jason's intentions wrongly. She evaluates Jason as a person by calling him a name, just as he called her a name.

Now let's fill in the particulars. By calling Sara a dingbat, Jason has revealed his impatience (an okay one-up type of feeling) but not his anxiety (a not-okay one-down feeling) about the test tomorrow. His intention is to get Sara to hurry up and pull herself together. And, too, there are probably some boy-girl anxieties in the background, barely, if at all, conscious. Dingbat is a teasing kind of name, not entirely without affectionate implications in its origin. Jason wants to show impatience, but not too roughly because in fact he likes Sara. But he doesn't want to act too gently, either, for if anyone found out he liked her he would be vulnerable to being teased himself; he would be one-down in a different game.

But Jason's sarcasm hurts Sara's feelings. She would like to be liked and admired even though she cannot seem to keep her Civil War battles straight. She thinks Jason meant to hurt her and put her down, because he is mean, aggressive, and a boy. She masks her hurt feelings with denial and disdain by calling Jason a creep. She wants to get even by making Jason feel small and ugly.

So the situation has escalated; the problem of covering the material in a limited time has blown up into an unpleasant personal confrontation. Jason's semi-serious, semi-teasing behavior puts Sara on the defensive and she retaliates in full anger. Now he will have to defend himself. Under such circumstances, what can the teacher do? As you remember, the group we observed and described in the previous chapter was able to move past their quarrel fairly quickly, without intervention, so that interference with the academic task was minimal. But suppose intervention is required. Then the teacher may decide simply to brush past the quarrel with a practical reminder of their task. On the other hand, he may decide it is time for these interpersonal difficulties to be faced directly. In this case he would attempt two things. First, he would guide the children to an awareness of the effects they are having on one another. Second, he would help them find better ways to express their feelings. His intervention might go something like this:

> Let's look at what happened. Jason said this, Sara replied that. Jason, how were you feeling when you called Sara a dingbat? Were you feeling mad?

> No . . . but she ought to hurry up, she ought to be organized by now.

> So you were feeling impatient?

> Yes.

> I bet you were also kind of worried about that test tomorrow. (This is said gently, with understanding, never in the tone of a cross-examination.)

> Yes.

But did teasing help Sara straighten things out?

In other words, the teacher is helping Jason focus on *his* feelings and *his* behavior, and moving away from examining what's wrong with Sara. The teacher may sense the boy-girl issue, but may want to save it for a later date when the children have more experience in sharing feelings and more confidence in expressing themselves. He then turns to Sara and asks how she felt when Jason called her a name. She may reply that she wanted to punch him in the mouth (a quick and common translation of feeling into fantasy action), but with help she may admit to feeling anger and finally to feeling hurt. This is because the teacher has, at least for the moment, converted a win-lose atmosphere into one where it is safe to share feelings of vulnerability. The teacher does this by his attitude as much as anything else, by being caring and helpful and gentle. Intervention of an authoritarian, one-up nature ("Why did you do that? It's not nice. I'm ashamed of you. You know better.") has the opposite effect. Of course they know better, but they are caught in some difficult emotions and do not know what else to do to get free.

Let us take a moment to clarify the theory underlying the mode of communication that we are recommending. We consider feelings to be more effective units of communication than name-calling. Why is this? There are two ways we commonly use the word "feel." First, we often say: I feel that you are an angry person, a wonderful fellow, or whatever. The "feeling" in this instance is really an opinion, my evaluation or judgment of you. But feeling has a more basic meaning: I feel angry, sad, annoyed, happy. Here I am not expressing an intellectual conclusion of some sort that turns the focus on you. I am expressing my own primary emotion. The focus is on "I," not you or "he" or "she." It is feeling in this sense that we think is the effective unit of communication for small-group problem solving, because it can be *heard* more easily by the recipient, and so is more easily dealt with. It does not arouse his or her defensiveness with the accompanying desire to run or to fight back. When I say that I am feeling angry, I am expressing a fact. I know my feelings, there is no guesswork involved, no theories about your character (for example: I "feel" that you are irresponsible). Now, if you want to interact with me, you will probably be interested in my feelings. You will want to determine whether or not you played any part in triggering them, since it would be useful (and perhaps necessary) to work this out before we can continue with our task. On the other hand, if I deliver a judgment about you instead of exposing my feelings, you will probably not be interested in anything but your own self-defense.

To return to our classroom example, once the feelings have been clarified, the teacher might have to reassure the children that it is all right to have "bad" feelings. He could point out that everyone does, and that it is legitimate to express anger or anxiety, but that there are ways to do it that are more constructive than others. If Sara had said outright: "I feel bad when you call me that" or "That makes me mad," Jason would have known immediately that his tactic of teasing was not having the effect he intended. Moreover, he would not have had to go on to prove he was not a creep. He could, of course, ignore Sara's protest. But at least he would have to ask himself, "Is that a good choice of behavior for what I want to accomplish?"[1]

The dialogue described above is, in fact, a rather idealized version of the process. It is usually not that quick or complete. But a hard-working group eventually reaches a point where interactions like this are neither impossible nor infrequent. One of the beauties of the small-group arrangement of a jigsaw classroom is that it provides the students with an opportunity for observing their own behavior as it affects others. It also provides opportunities for learning how to handle feelings of anger, impatience, shyness, or affection. Importantly, this learning occurs while the students are learning about the Civil War or the poetry of Emily Dickenson. The learning of communication skills is not a separate lesson in a jigsaw classroom. Rather, it enhances the mastery of the content at hand, increasing the usefulness and attentiveness of the human resources involved.

NOTE

1. For a more detailed analysis of communication skills, see Chapter 8 in *The Social Animal* by Elliot Aronson (W. H. Freeman, 1976).

Problems Facing the Jigsaw Teacher **6**

*I*n recent years, the jigsaw method has been introduced into a number of classrooms. While our research continues to point out the advantages of jigsaw learning, certain problems do occur for which jigsaw teachers are devising a variety of solutions. This chapter contains a disparate collection of some of the more common problems, together with suggestions for how they might be handled. Many of these problems are not unique to the jigsaw method. But, as we saw earlier, the jigsaw method often illuminates problems that are hidden in the more competitive classroom dynamics. More importantly, though, the jigsaw method often provides possible solutions that otherwise would be less readily available.

The first problem we will explore is a good example of the last point. How do we help the poor reader, the child who may be reading one or several grade levels below her peers, and who, consequently, is suffering both in practical and emotional terms?

THE POOR READER

The reading ability of the students in a single jigsaw group may vary considerably. In the competitive classroom, the poor readers can be "tracked," thus making it very much "their" problem and insulating the other students from them. But in a jigsaw group, some group members will inevitably find themselves dependent for vital information on a student who, because of reading problems, cannot easily get that information to them. The problem for that relatively unskilled student is not only that he cannot read very well but also that he cannot hide the fact from his peers as he might have been able to do in a more traditional classroom. He is confronted with their impatience and their unfavorable judgments. As a result he is under pressure which potentially could inhibit his performance still further.

There are several tactics a teacher can adopt in order to forestall such a destructive situation while at the same time increasing the flexibility of the learning environment. In a jigsaw group, anyone can make a useful contribution. For example, the slower reader may be given a drawing assignment, or the teacher can assign material of different reading levels to each group, making sure that the less accomplished readers get the least difficult material. Often the teacher will compose original material for the poorest readers instead of merely reproducing a unit from a text where vocabulary and concepts are set at too high a grade level. Material may also be recorded on cassettes. The recording may be assigned to the quicker students to encourage in them a sense of responsibility toward their less skilled peers, while keeping them busy and challenged with an interesting, constructive task. Generally the recorded material is used in conjunction with, not instead of, written material in order to reinforce orally what the child is reading.

Another practice that jigsaw teachers have employed with great frequency and success is that of student coaching with the higher-achieving students working directly with the slower students. This practice is more desirable than that of isolating a student with a tape recorder because it is yet another way to stress the development of interpersonal skills. The coaching teams are set up within each jigsaw group and serve to underscore its supportive values and the interdependency of the students. As we noted in our discussion of group composition, the benefits are mutual. The adept reader has the immediate, energizing reward of an image change: that is, he sees himself as a helper instead of as a hampered and bored student. The slower reader is being helped by someone who is more skilled but not perfect, a role model within the limits of possible attainment, compared, for example, to the teacher, who is a know-every-thing of almost super-human ability. In our experience, this procedure opens the slower reader to learning by reducing his need to feel intimidated and defensive. This, in turn, frees him to be more attentive and take more risks in his learning.

When the jigsaw process is first getting under way, the teacher will probably be the one to suggest the coaching arrangement. Eventually, as cooperation becomes an established practice, the students themselves will make the choice to work in this manner. At first it is easier to imagine a faster student offering to help than it is to imagine a slower student taking the initiative to ask for that help. However, the kind of classroom the jigsaw teacher is developing is one where all the students realize that different levels of skills at any given moment are ordinary facts of life, a cause for neither shame nor vanity. As competitive pressures yield, this does tend to happen. The slower students or poorer readers often become quite accurate judges of what they can and cannot do, and are not too embarrassed to ask for help when they need it.

Once the coaching team is set up, the teacher helps the students make effective use of one another as resources. He shows them how to break a task into parts and also provides a structure for their interaction. For example, he might suggest that David first read the paragraph to Susan. Having heard the words and the rhythmical phrasing that serves to clarify content, Susan could then read the passage back. Then together they could decide on two important points and discuss how Susan is going to present them. As the teacher moves from group to group, he will want to be particularly attentive to how the coaching process is functioning. Is David getting a little dictatorial, for example, teaching down to Susan rather than working with her? The teacher may also ask the students to comment on the process: Does David find that teaching the material helps him to learn it? How does Susan think the system is working for her? Does she have any suggestions for David that would enable him to be more helpful to her? The sooner the slower students are encouraged to state their own needs and opinions, the more their self-esteem grows, along with a sense that they have some control over their learning.

Providing a variety of materials and arranging for student coaches are two strategies for helping poor readers that have worked in jigsaw classrooms, but of course they are not unique to the jigsaw approach; they can be employed in any classroom structure. Now let us look at a solution that is unique to the jigsaw procedure; indeed, it forms a basic part of its structure. We call this the counterpart group. Suppose that all jigsaw groups in a classroom are working on the same unit, for example, Spanish Explorers. Soon after the written material is handed out, the teacher restructures the groups temporarily so that the students with the same piece of the puzzle form new groups, counterpart groups, to help each other learn their part of the material. That is, all the children who were dealt Magellan form into a Magellan counterpart group, as do the children who have Cortez, and so forth. In this way, poorer readers are again being helped by their peers, this time members of other groups who are responsible for the same section. The students in a counterpart group have a chance to hear the material read, are helped with the meanings of words, can share examples, and can try out their presentations. When the original jigsaw groups resume, even the slowest student has his section fairly well planned and rehearsed. Through this procedure he gains confidence. He begins to see himself as a useful member of his jigsaw group rather than the "dummy."

Counterpart groups have additional advantages. For instance, they permit a cross fertilization of ideas as well as of skills. Even the brightest student is stimulated by the questions, examples, and trial presentations of his counterparts. They give each other ideas about explaining material in different ways. The counterpart group may also be considered an effective device to remedy listlessness on one of those dull, low-energy days that descend from time to time on every classroom. A typical jigsaw group runs for a period of six to ten weeks, long enough so that the children in it may occasionally get bored with each other and may want the excitement of a temporary change in routine. On the other hand, they may decidedly not want such a change because they have become so comfortable with their teammates;

they know exactly what to expect of each other and patterns of interaction have become established and easy. In either case, the counterpart group challenges them to make new interpersonal adaptations without disrupting the smoothly functioning jigsaw learning group. Finally, as jigsaw group identity solidifies, the groups may be tempted to view each other competitively. Temporary restructuring with counterpart groups builds bonds across groups, thus helping to keep such intergroup competition from becoming pervasive.

There is, however, a problem with counterpart groups. The children may not immediately be comfortable working with each other, particularly when the jigsaw process is new to them. They may even have difficulty getting organized and down to work. Teachers generally find it advisable to pick a responsible and capable leader even for these temporary groups. It is also helpful, on occasion, to run through a quick teambuilding exercise to establish a cooperative mood. Once the jigsaw process becomes familiar, cooperative attitudes tend to carry over from group to group.

THE "TROUBLE MAKER"

Inevitably in almost any classroom there will be a student who, in relation to his classmates, is immature or recalcitrant. Such a student is commonly called a "trouble maker." In a jigsaw classroom we would be surprised if there were not at least one or two students who simply will not work effectively in a group or who may even go so far as to sabotage efforts at cooperation by persistent attempts at mischief. For example, Steve may have a game he likes to play: when Jean is making her presentation, Steve makes the others laugh by mimicking her facial expressions and gestures. The leader calls him on it, not for the first time. And, also not for the first time, Steve says, with wide-eyed innocence, that he wasn't doing anything —Allison was. Steve's repeated "sneak and defense" behavior might be an important survival tactic that he has developed at home, or it may simply be an attention-getting device. Whatever its cause, it is destructive to the group and he is exerting a powerful disruptive influence. Moreover, he is not learning anything. It would be a mistake simply to thrust Steve into a jigsaw group without preparation. Students like Steve may need to work alone for a while under close adult supervision. Teachers we have worked with have made it clear to the recalcitrant student that working in a jigsaw group is an opportunity to be earned. The student can do this by making responsible decisions about his learning situation. For example, with teacher guidance, Steve may draw up a daily contract. He may agree (1) to learn the new words on page 7 and (2) to write a short paragraph on each explorer. It is impressed upon him that these are the tasks to which he is committed. The teacher then begins to introduce him to cooperative activities. Perhaps he and another carefully chosen student are assigned to make a chart for the class. The point is, teachers find it wise to bring the Steves in their classrooms step by step toward the goal of group participation. To leave him in a group and hope for the best can be disruptive to him and to the others. On the other hand, to haul him out of the group is punishing and humiliating. Thus it is more constructive to try to spot him in the weeks before jigsawing begins and to communicate to him at that time that jigsawing is an earned opportunity. Then when Steve sits down with the teacher to design an "independent study" program for himself, chances are that he will not feel he is being left out or stigmatized because he is some sort of bad person. Rather, it is our experience that he will understand that he simply has certain things to accomplish before he can join the others. By the time he is ready to join, the jigsaw groups will have begun to work smoothly and he, watching from the outside, sees it as something that looks like fun. We have found that creative teachers, far from allowing a recalcitrant student to undermine a jigsaw group, have succeeded in using the jigsaw group to expedite the learning of pro-social behavior among their less mature students.

MATERIALS

Perhaps the most difficult problem new jigsaw teachers face is that of obtaining and developing appropriate instructional materials. The usual curriculum material must be divided into segments for the students to share. Some assignments have to be created from various resources, others can simply be reproduced from texts. Everything must be transferred to cards that can be handed out once class begins (see Appendix B for sample material). This requires time, which becomes an increasingly precious and scarce commodity as the school year progresses. More specifically, it requires the *efficient use* of time. When we get rushed, we tend to plan less and to be less systematic while just the opposite behavior is the most efficient.

The ideal time for a teacher to prepare a curriculum is when he is under no pressure to teach it, such as during vacations, and this is when most teachers do it. Under such relaxed conditions the task becomes a creative, enjoyable experience instead of a discouraging burden. A unit that is only half prepared frustrates a teacher: "If only I had had a little more time . . ." It also can frustrate the students and interfere with the smooth functioning of the jigsaw process.

However, advance preparation is easier said than done. But teachers themselves have learned to cooperate at this task. Often several teachers in the same school or district work together to prepare material and, once school has started, continue to share supervisory responsibilities, meeting regularly to assess what seems to be working and what does not, whether there was too much material for that week's assignment or too little, and so forth. A team of teachers not only decreases the work load but also eliminates the loneliness that can develop when one is attempting innovation.

There may be instances when the students themselves can help in the physical preparation of a unit, transferring material to cards, cutting a mimeo into strips, and gathering illustrations. In some classrooms, a jigsaw group has been assigned the entire responsibility for a unit. In such a case, the students would devise the assignments, decide how to divide and distribute the reading material, and create questions and exercises. This kind of organizing activity is a very effective way to learn material, as teachers know from their own experience when, for example, they discover the Civil War they have managed to avoid for a lifetime is coming up in the next chapter of the seventh-grade text. However, to be able to shoulder such a responsibility in a cooperative effort, the students should have some experience in the group-process techniques of jigsawing. Thus, a unit on curriculum planning might best be left until spring.

Finally, there are organizations in the country, such as the Educational Development Corporation in Massachusetts, which design curriculum material to be learned in small cooperative groups. While the breakdown in activities would not necessarily follow a jigsaw pattern, there are some units in science or social science that could be easily adapted. The curriculum supervisors of a district will often know what group materials are available for each subject and level.

POTENTIAL PROBLEMS
WITH OTHER SCHOOL PERSONNEL

Picture this scene. Children are scattered about the room. Everybody is talking at once. Chaos. And the principal walks in! What is she likely to conclude? That the teacher must be an undisciplined person, unskilled, ineffective, for how can children learn anything in such a noisy atmosphere? Or perhaps the teacher does not care, is sacrificing academics and good citizenship to some vague ideal of spontaneity.

Such might also be the thoughts of a non-jigsaw teacher upon observing a jigsaw classroom for the first time. New techniques often push us to defend our way and finding fault with others makes our way look comparatively better. And, in fact, the jigsaw classroom is noisier than a traditional one. But there is noise that is just noise, and there is the kind of noise which many experienced teachers would describe as the sounds of living and learning. An outsider to the jigsaw method may believe he is witnessing chaos. In reality he is observing creative energy released by a carefully planned structure, not energy combatting structure. The observer needs to be told what is going on.

Jigsaw teachers have found it useful to prepare their supervisors and colleagues for their classroom innovations. They have learned that it facilitates understanding when they describe the technique in full, stressing that it encourages student responsibility while in no way reducing the teacher's work. As for good citizenship and academic achievement, the goals of jigsaw teachers are no different from those of their colleagues. To defuse tensions further and even to gather suggestions, some teachers ask their colleagues to sit in on a jigsaw group and then share their opinions as to the effectiveness of the technique in teaching the content material. All too often, classrooms and their teachers are isolated units in the school. In some schools teachers are colleagues only insofar as they hold the same degrees and work in the same building. For a jigsaw teacher to open her method to discussion gives some substance to the word "colleague." It might even stimulate the faculty to form into a kind of learning group where the value of interdependence is stressed. Where there is input and feedback, where all opinions are sought and respected, competition between teaching styles tends to diminish.

Students too must be able to articulate class objectives to outsiders, particularly to those parents who say, "That's not the way we did things in my day!" To this end, teachers and students often develop a routine for welcoming visitors and showing them around. However, the students are discouraged from comparing their class too favorably to other classes since this only arouses animosity and competitiveness.

The ultimate proof of any pudding, of course, is in the eating. The jigsaw technique works—not simply in improving human relations but in improving classroom and exam performance. Moreover, unlike some other innovative procedures (such as the open classroom), students are learning virtually the same material as their peers in more competitive classrooms. Thus the teacher is not dependent on our data (discussed in Chapter 7) to provide support for her contention that the jigsaw method works. Rather, the academic performance of her classroom is directly comparable to that of her more typical colleague across the hall. And the proof of her contention that jigsaw students perform as well or better than others can be readily demonstrated by comparing exam performances after about eight weeks of jigsawing.

MAINTAINING A COOPERATIVE SPIRIT

There are times even among experienced jigsaw groups when the cooperative spirit seems to dissipate and the students lose interest. The jigsaw teacher is concerned with keeping alive a more enjoyable, more productive, and supportive mood. We mentioned earlier that a change of routine by setting up counterpart groups can be helpful. In addition, one fifth-grade teacher begins each new unit (for which new groups are usually formed) with teambuilding exercises, and once every few weeks begins the jigsaw hour with some variation on the Broken Squares exercise described in Chapter 2. This takes only five minutes, at the end of which time the students are ready to work more closely with each other. Some teachers have discovered stories or parables which inspire their students and build cooperative spirit;[1] storytelling can teach and relax at the same time.

TEACHER DISCOURAGEMENT

We have been concentrating thus far on how to help the students. Who helps the helper? Teachers get discouraged for any number of reasons during the course of a school year. This is especially so when they are initiating a new method—the pressure of new responsibilities, the insecurity of not knowing in advance what will and will not work. The advice we are about to discuss can be used effectively by any teacher using almost any technique, but the jigsaw teachers we have worked with have found it particularly helpful.

For example, there is some guilt or anxiety reported by most skilled teachers, reflected in their tendency to demand perfection of themselves 100 percent of the time. They fall into a slump, the bad day or week is all their fault, they are not reaching one or two students who are having trouble. Anybody who is discouraged feels better if he can talk about it. It may seem functional for a teacher to be able to let off steam in the faculty lounge. Unfortunately, this is not a helpful tactic if it stimulates a general "gripe session." For example, a teacher who is momentarily discouraged may mention a student who was very disruptive that particular morning, which may elicit a volley of stories that begin, "If you think that's bad, let me tell you the trouble *I'm* having." After a session of this sort, when the teachers return to their classrooms they are likely to feel even worse and to wish they did not have to face those awful children again.

Much more helpful than a casual coffee group complaining together is a group of colleagues set up explicitly as a support system. In our experience with teachers using the jigsaw technique, those who were happiest and got the most out of it were the ones who were able to form a group for mutual support and consultation. Members not only support each other emotionally, but encourage rational problem solving. They set up norms to give teachers energy and direction, and they devise a systematic method for exploring new alternatives. Being a good consultant is itself a skill, but one that can be easily acquired.

The effective consultant hears her fellow teacher out, listens supportively, and then asks the kinds of questions that will clarify issues and generate possible solutions. Sometimes the discouraged teacher states explicitly the kind of help he is looking for. For example, he might say he is in a slump and simply wants to unburden himself. Could his colleague listen for a few minutes and say back to him what she thinks she hears him saying? Even when the teacher does not quite know what he wants, it can be very helpful to have the gist of one's own words played back by a consultant. "I guess I really am saying that. Maybe that's the heart of the problem." Then they might go on to consider the questions he could usefully ask himself in order to begin shaping a solution.

To illustrate: Carol is a student who is falling behind. Her teacher is particularly upset because Carol had started the year full of excitement and hope; this year, in this classroom, she was really going to work hard and learn something. The teacher believes he has failed her somehow. Has he? While his feelings are painful and worthy of sympathy, his question is not a particularly fruitful one in practical terms. So after acknowledging his feelings, the consultant might encourage him to ask himself:

What specific learning problems does Carol have? What does the record say? What do I know about her attitudes? How could the technique we're using (jigsaw or whatever) be affecting her difficulties? Such questions developed and examined with trusted colleagues will benefit Carol. And, very importantly, because these questions are infused with practical energy, because they reflect the teacher's power to analyze and understand a problem and to be of specific use, they benefit him by allaying his fears and combatting discouragement: there *is* something he can do. In sum, while a support system gives a teacher some opportunity to vent feelings and to have a sense of being heard, most of the time is spent on specifically defining a problem and thinking about different ways to solve it.

NOTE

1. There are two stories we know of that in a lyrical and subtle manner illustrate the fact that as different as we may be in terms of height, weight, race, religion, ethnicity, and so forth, there is a special beauty about being human that transcends and is enriched by these differences. The stories imply that as we pay attention to what is essential in the other person, we see her beauty more clearly. One of these stories, "The Superlative Animal," can be found on pages 4-5 of the Bantam edition of J. D. Salinger's *Raise High the Roofbeam, Carpenter*. The other is on pages 11-14 of the Collier edition of Alan Watt's *The Book*.

The Jigsaw Technique in Action: Research Findings **7**

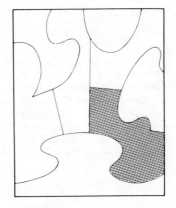

*A*fter only a few weeks of utilizing the jigsaw technique, it was abundantly clear to most of the teachers in our project that it was working. Most experienced teachers do not need complex statistical analyses, charts, graphs, or numerical tables in order to assess the viability of an instructional technique. They are sensitive to subtle changes in the classroom atmosphere and to relatively minor improvements in the performance and attitude of individual students. Moreover, in many of the classrooms some rather dramatic events occurred which sold the teachers on jigsawing before we, as investigators, began to collate and analyze our data. Indeed, one of the most gratifying aspects of the entire project for us was listening to the excitement of many of the teachers as they spontaneously shared classroom anecdotes and success stories with us—long before the "final returns were in."

For example, Mrs. T., a teacher in Austin, Texas, was beaming as she told us of the time that the brightest student in her class made this important discovery: "You know, Mrs. T, I used to think that Paul was dumb—but now I know that he really tries."

A teacher from Santa Cruz, California, sent us the following vignettes:

"*Charles R:* Charles came about a month or two after school started, fairly low academically. He had a horrible time just staying in his other classes; he was always out wandering around. He could not attend to a task. He had quite a bit of trouble on the playground getting along with other kids. Then we initiated the jigsaw technique. From the very beginning, the jigsaw technique was perfect for Charles. Even though he scored low in reading, he learned the material very fast after hearing it read once. Since jigsawing involves some movement and a lot of conversation, I rarely had to go hunting for Charles in the halls. Jigsawing gave him a chance to be the focal point of at least five other students' attention. . . . Any other kind of social studies technique, such as strictly reading and writing, or even whole class simulation games (where he would always want to be center of attention), simply wouldn't work with Charles. But because of jigsaw, Charles and I developed a good relationship; I didn't have to be nagging him all the time.

"Bill G: Bill was seen in his other classes as a "mess-off." By putting him in a team situation (thus separating him from some of his closest friends), he was forced into working with a completely new group of people. We discovered a great leadership quality that had been hidden before.

"Peter W: Peter is very conscientious and responsible. He has some difficulty reading. Peter was extremely worried about the effect each quiz would have on his grade. His first question was always, 'What if I flunk?' Being a member of a jigsaw team really helped him deal with that fear. The other members of the team helped him learn the material and gave him support and the assurance that he would not flunk."

In another school, several of the teachers proudly told us that their pupils' change in attitude generalized to other classes throughout the school. For example, both the music and P.E. teachers complimented the jigsaw teachers on their students' behavior, mentioning that the students as a whole had become noticeably more cooperative and considerate. Since the music and P.E. teachers were not involved in the jigsaw project and were not even aware that anything different was happening in the regular classrooms, it was particularly exciting to the classroom teachers that a major change had been discerned.

These are the things that matter to teachers: changes in student behavior, attitudes, and performance. So, with testimony like this to fall back on, why should we bother to do systematic research? Isn't first-hand experience all that matters? Not quite. It is conceivable that individual teachers, because of their commitment to the project and general agreement with our goals, may do some unconscious editing—emphasizing positive incidents and relegating negative ones to the back burners of their memory. Moreover, it is possible that exceptional progress can indeed occur in a few classrooms, but it may be due to special circumstances that have little or nothing to do with the jigsaw technique itself. In these cases it would be erroneous to conclude that the jigsaw technique is effective when perhaps it is not.

For these reasons, it is essential to have independent, well controlled research data; that is what we will examine in this chapter.[1] Although in our technical reports of this research we have tended to focus on numbers and statistics, we hope not to lose sight of the fact that education is for individuals. The goal of this research is to determine systematically whether or not the jigsaw technique is a valuable way to educate the individual students.

The research that we conducted on jigsaw groups grew, in part, out of our own ideas about education. However, no research project comes entirely from the heads of those who design it. In the first chapter, we talked about how our concern about the extreme consequences of competitiveness—especially as it was manifested in newly desegregated schools—led to the development of the jigsaw technique. While this is accurate, it is also true that many of our ideas were influenced by the research that other scientists have conducted while exploring the place of cooperation and competition in the classroom. First we will review some of this work; then we will show how our research fits into this line of investigation. Finally we will describe exactly how we conducted our research and the results we obtained.

PREVIOUS RESEARCH

As far back as 1937, educators Stuart Courtis, E. T. McSwain, and Nellie Morrison suggested that teachers could practice cooperative techniques in the classroom. Their book was a harbinger of the work that was to come later when social scientists began to investigate systematically the role and effects of cooperation and competition in the educational process. There was a major impetus to this research in 1949 when Morton Deutsch began to specify the kinds of relationships people would be likely to have as a result of cooperative or competitive interactions. According to Deutsch, the critical difference between cooperation and competition lies in the result of the interaction between two or more people: with cooperation, individuals have the same outcome; with competition, individuals have different outcomes. Specifically, if we cooperate, when you win, I win too. When you lose, I lose also. But if we compete, when you win, I lose; when you lose, I win.

Let's look at Deutsch's ideas a little more closely, using the popular competitive game of tennis as an example. If you and I play a game of tennis, my goal is to hit the ball within bounds. Another equally important goal for me is to hit the ball so that you cannot reach it. In competitive tennis all of my energies are directed toward making the game difficult for you. Whenever I score a point, I am pleased. When you score a point, my reaction is likely to be different. It is possible that if you should win, I would be jealous, embarrassed, disappointed, or even angry. Of course, the use of competition in a game like tennis has positive as well as negative aspects. Games of tennis among acquaintances usually are played in a friendly manner, where keeping score serves primarily to increase interest in the game. In such a case the positive aspects of competition almost always outweigh the negative ones.

In a cooperative version of tennis, you and I would still be on opposite sides of a tennis court, but we would be trying to see how many consecutive times we could rally the ball over the net. In this version of the game, it is important for me to hit the ball so that you can reach it and return it. When you return the ball to me, I am happy for you. Both of us benefit. My energies are now directed toward making the game easier for you so we can continue to play. I am working just as hard to do my best as I did in the competitive game. Only my goal has changed.[2]

Deutsch suggested that because of the different natures of the outcomes of cooperation and competition, the participants will have a different type of relationship in each situation. People who cooperate will be inclined to be interested in each other's welfare, will be trusting and open with one another, and will receive satisfaction from their partner's successes. By contrast, people who compete will be inclined to have antagonistic interests, will be suspicious and hostile toward each other, and will have an exploitative attitude toward their partner. The different kinds of tennis games suggest how these different reactions might occur.

Deutsch tested these ideas in his own college classrooms. He induced the students in some of his classes to cooperate by giving them problems to solve together for a group grade. In other classes, he induced the students to compete by giving them problems to solve alone for individual grades. He found that his cooperative groups were higher in coordinated efforts, friendliness, and attentiveness than were his competitive groups. Two years later, Donald Haines and W. J. McKeachie also studied the effect of cooperation and competition on college students. They compared cooperative and competitive class discussion methods in psychology courses to determine their effects on the students' anxiety, achievement, and satisfaction. In competitive discussion groups, the students became more anxious, were less able to perform well in discussion, were less self-assured, and became dissatisfied with the group. Students in cooperative discussion groups, however, were more relaxed and effective in the discussions, and enjoyed the discussions more.

Other researchers have found similar results in elementary school classrooms. Celia Stendler, Dara Damrin, and Aleyne Haines found that second-graders who were painting a mural engaged in more "positive" behavior when there was a group reward than when there were individual rewards. Positive behavior meant engaging in friendly conversation, such as giving praise, suggestions, and encouragement to others, as well as sharing materials and helping others. Beeman Phillips and Louis D'Amico studied fourth-graders' liking for one another when they worked in either cooperative or competitive groups at a task requiring the children to identify animals by asking questions. In the cooperative groups the children in each group shared equally in the group's reward, regardless of who had gotten the most points. In the competitive groups the rewards were unequal, with the greatest rewards going to those children who had the most points. In the cooperative groups the children grew to like each other better during the course of the group interaction. This did not occur in the competitive groups.

In addition to the research mentioned above, popular writers such as John Holt, Neil Postman, and Charles Weingartner have reached large audiences of educators, as well as the general public, with the message that a strictly competitive environment is not the best one for students. You might be asking yourself, if there is so much evidence that cooperation has positive effects in the classroom, why hasn't it been used more? The problem that educators have experienced in applying the findings of the research on cooperation has been in discovering a method that can be used in the ongoing curriculum. In the typical research study, a team of outsiders enters the classroom, makes some changes in a small part of the classroom activities, and conducts the research. Then, after a short period of time, the researchers leave, sometimes without even sharing the results of the study. More frequently, results are discussed but the teacher does not receive sufficient training to allow him or her to utilize the new technique fully. Under these circumstances it has been almost impossible for teachers to sustain any changes that have occurred during the research period. Understandably, the researcher who has been interested in studying the effectiveness of a particular technique has not focused his or her attention on the needs of adapting that technique to a particular classroom. Just as understandably, those classroom needs have been the primary interest on the part of teachers hoping for more practical information from the researchers.

One of the major purposes for our own study was to fill both needs simultaneously. We designed a careful scientific study so that we could assess whether or not our technique worked. It was our aim to be as meticulous as possible so that the results of our work could bear up under the careful scrutiny of our most sophisticated scientific colleagues. At the same time, we made every endeavor to develop a program and a set of techniques that a teacher could apply to the classroom and explain to other teachers. Thus, although we are interested in the scientific results of this study, we are equally interested in planting the seed of jigsaw groups and helping them grow and spread from classroom to classroom.

We have mentioned how earlier research on the use of co-operative techniques in the classroom has influenced our own research. There is a second line of research that has influenced our thinking about ways of learning in the classroom. This is peer teaching: the effects of one student teaching another student. A research team headed by Ronald Lippitt has studied several peer-teaching programs, finding that both the "tutor" and the "pupil" are helped by peer teaching. The tutors showed improved attitudes and interest in school, increased ability to work cooperatively with other children, and increased self-respect and belief in their own ability. Both tutors and pupils showed academic gains. In another investigation, Robert Cloward studied minority fifth- and sixth-grade students who were deficient in reading skills. He too found that both tutors and pupils increased in reading skills.

THE JIGSAW PILOT STUDY

We combined these two successful techniques, cooperation and peer-teaching, in our research. This was done by putting students in cooperative (jigsaw) groups where each student would have the opportunity to be both the teacher and the learner. To see if our ideas were feasible, some of us conducted a two-week exploratory study before launching the full-scale investigation. In the initial study, students in two fifth-grade classrooms were divided into learning groups of five to six students. Half of the groups were taught by a teacher. The other half were taught by students in the jigsaw manner. In the latter groups, each student had a segment of the assignment that no other student had. As mentioned in the first chapter, this was done by dividing the assignment into pieces, like a jigsaw puzzle. Each student taught his or her piece of information to the other students in the group. That way, each student had to learn what each other member of the group was teaching in order to learn the entire lesson for the day.

At several points in the study, we measured the students' liking for one another to see if it changed as a result of the type of learning groups. Just prior to the beginning of the study, there were no differences in liking ratings expressed by the students for their group members. However, at the halfway point in this study, members of the jigsaw groups liked each other more than members of the teacher-taught groups did. At this point the teacher-taught groups were placed into the jigsaw environment; that is, they became student-taught groups. At the end of the study, liking ratings were again the same among all groups: liking ratings among those formerly teacher-taught (now jigsaw) groups were now as high as the liking ratings among the original jigsaw groups. We concluded that the jigsaw technique had caused an increase in liking within the groups. Further, we were able to see that simply working in small learning groups was not sufficient to increase liking among members of the groups. It was not until the teacher-taught groups became jigsaw groups that the liking ratings for members of those groups increased.

Encouraged by the results of this small study, we conducted a full-scale project in collaboration with the participating teachers. In the next few sections we will present the design of our study and the results that we found. First, let's see, on the basis of the research we have presented in this chapter, what predictions we were able to make about what we would find in our larger study.

(1) We expected that students in jigsaw groups would like their group-mates more than the rest of their classmates.

(2) We also expected that, compared to students in traditional classrooms, students in jigsaw classrooms would

(a) Like school more.

(b) Increase more in self-esteem.

(c) Decrease in feelings of competitiveness.

(d) Believe more that they could learn from other children.

OUR FULL-SCALE JIGSAW RESEARCH

Now you have some background for our research: what other investigators have learned about cooperation and competition; our pilot study; and the results we were hoping to obtain in the full-scale study.

At this point, you may be wondering why we even bothered to do the larger study. With so much previous research pointing to the usefulness of cooperation in the classroom and with the results of the pilot jigsaw study, why was anything else needed? Wasn't there already sufficient proof that a cooperative technique like jigsaw groups would be beneficial to students? The teachers and students in the pilot study liked the jigsaw groups and there were positive effects on students' liking for one another. Why not push ahead to implement this innovation and let more students benefit? At this stage, research may seem like needless waste of time. And indeed this is exactly what happens with many educational innovations: the initial experiences of teachers and students look promising, so the innovation is touted publicly and adopted widely; only later, if ever, is it adequately researched.

Put yourself in the position of the classroom teacher. You have just heard about some "fantastic" new teaching method that is supposed to solve nearly all classroom problems. And you have heard about the experiences of enthusiastic teachers who have tried the method and think it to be marvelous. You have heard of such methods lots of times, and in fact some of them have been effective. But often they have failed you, and you have been left disappointed, wishing you could somehow have known more specifically beforehand just what the effects might be. The problem with far too many educational innovations is that there is little or no systematic evaluation to see if they are really as effective as the enthusiastic supporters say they are.

It is much like looking for a simple, useful weight-reducing diet. Several have been written about, but we don't know if any of them have been thoroughly tested. The claims sound good, but which one is really going to work? This is akin to the teacher's quandary. Innovative teaching methods look and sound promising, but it is hard to know what their actual effect in the classroom is likely to be. What is worse, unless there is solid evidence showing how effective any particular method is, a teacher may commit himself to one when there are even better methods available. For these reasons, we felt it was as essential to evaluate the effects of the jigsaw method as it was to try to develop it fully.

How can teaching methods be evaluated? A frequently used way is simply to ask the teachers, students, or administrators involved to give some report about the method's effectiveness. After all, who knows better than the participants what the effects really are? But this approach also has problems, most obviously that the participants may be biased. If the method happens to fit their own style or personality they may over-praise it; if not, they may seriously underrate it. Further, a teacher's positive or negative reaction may have more to do with her own teaching style, or the type of students being taught, than with the merits of the method itself. In any case, useful information may be hard to find.

The most reliable way to ensure an unbiased evaluation is to conduct some kind of carefully controlled research. By carefully controlled, we mean primarily that (1) the problems to be researched have been formulated beforehand and (2) by using questionnaires or other research instruments, the data from persons experiencing the new method can be compared with data (also from the same instruments) from persons who are not experiencing the new method. Comparison groups are called "control groups" and are used in all types of scientific research. In the current study, the control group consisted of classrooms where students were not divided into jigsaw groups; the teachers, not the students, did most of the teaching and the atmosphere was that found in normally competitive classrooms. We will refer to these as control classes.

Since the control classes were an essential part of our study, the control teachers were selected as carefully as the jigsaw teachers. It was important that both groups of teachers be competent and highly committed to their methods of teaching. One possibility would have been to select our control group from among the teachers who had volunteered to try our method, but we rejected this idea. Since the teachers were all volunteering to learn a new technique, we assumed that they might not be strongly committed to their present style of teaching and felt that they might not try very hard if asked to continue in the same old way; we wanted good teachers who also liked what they were doing. Moreover, since we wanted to have control teachers and jigsaw teachers from the same schools and the same grade levels, we asked the jigsaw teachers to give us the names of grade-level colleagues whom they considered to be as competent as they themselves were but who were committed to and happy with more typical teaching techniques. It was these teachers, then, who were asked to participate in the study as controls. To have secured control teachers who were less committed or less effective than the jigsaw teachers would have been tantamount to stacking the deck in our favor, rendering the control groups useless for scientific comparison.

With our research, we were trying to determine the effect the jigsaw groups had upon students' attitudes as well as upon their liking for one another. To do this, we developed a series of hypotheses, each of which was designed to answer a specific question about the effects of the jigsaw method. For each hypothesis we predicted a particular result. In addition, we worded each hypothesis in a way that allowed us to compare our findings from the jigsaw classes with the findings from the competitive classes.

An example is our hypothesis stating that students in jigsaw classes would like school more than students in control classes. Since we had tried to arrange things so that these two types of classes were as similar as possible, except that the jigsaw classes contained cooperative groups, we knew that any differences in our findings could be attributed to the effect of the cooperative groups.

To assess the effect of the jigsaw groups, we designed a twenty-two-item questionnaire to measure a student's attitudes toward school and toward herself. We also designed a second questionnaire to measure each student's liking for each of her classmates. In order to be able to determine if there were changes over time attributable to the jigsaw groups, we needed to know about attitudes and liking at several points in time.

For that reason, we administered the two questionnaires at the beginning of the study, to measure attitudes and liking before the study began, and at the end of six weeks. We did this in both the control and the jigsaw classrooms.

In both types of classes, the questionnaires were administered in the same way, according to a standardized script. For the attitude questionnaire, each of the twenty-two questions was read aloud twice, and students were asked to indicate their answers by marking one of seven boxes of increasing size under each question. Accompanying each box was a verbal description of the meaning of that box. For example, this is how the first question looked:

"How much do you like school this year?"

□	□	□	□	□	□	□
like not at all	like very, very little	like very little	like some	like a lot	like very much	like very, very much

If a student did not like school at all, he was asked to check the smallest box on the left. But if he did not dislike school entirely or liked it only a very small amount, he was asked to check the next-to-smallest box, and so on, until the largest box, which a student would check if he liked school very, very much. Thus, the boxes provided a "picture" of the increasing degree of feeling represented by the verbal labels underneath each box. We found this way of presenting the questions to be very helpful for students who had difficulty in reading.

We measured the children's liking for one another in a somewhat different manner, by presenting the students with a fantasy trip. Specifically, the students were asked to imagine taking a trip to an exciting island. We told them that they could take their classmates with them but that they had to make the trip in a small boat, and although the boat could carry only a few classmates at a time, eventually, with enough trips, the entire class could come to the island. We asked the students to assign numbers to each of their classmates, the numbers indicating how soon they wanted each classmate to join them on the island. The numbers ranged from seven to one, seven being the number assigned to classmates the student wanted most to be with and who could go over on the first boatload. Classmates given the number six would be able to go to the island on the second boatload, and so on. We assumed that these preferences mirrored the students' liking for those classmates. Each student was given a roster listing all the people in the class and asked to place a number from seven to one beside each name.

We might have asked the students simply to tell us whom they did and did not like, which would have done away with the complexity and labor that we imposed on ourselves with the rigmarole of the fantasy trip. In fact, we thought about doing just that. But advice from the teachers changed our minds. They feared that asking children to state liking and disliking outright might create discomfort and hurt feelings among the students. We became convinced that this was an unacceptable manner of gathering information about students' liking for one another. In conducting this research, our highest priority was that our data gathering would cause neither physical nor emotional disruption in the classroom. The teachers felt that a much more reasonable way to secure sociometric data would be to devise a strategy that would be pleasant for the students, while yielding valuable data. With these purposes in mind, the fantasy boat trip to the island emerged as our method.

We did not want students in the jigsaw classes to realize that the questionnaires were related in any way to the fact that they were working in groups because we were afraid that this knowledge might affect the way they answered the questions, thus distorting our results. For this reason, students in both the jigsaw and control classes were told that the questionnaires were part of a study of the entire school system and that fifth-grade students in many other schools were also answering the same questionnaires. Another factor is important: the persons administering the questionnaires took special care not to show the students' answers to their teachers. Accordingly, students in both jigsaw and control classes could be assured that their answers were confidential.

As you can see, the major part of our research was concerned with the answers that students in both types of classes gave each time the questionnaires were administered. We also needed to have a reasonably clear idea of what was taking place in each of the classrooms. In order to be certain that any changes in attitudes or liking were due to the effect of the jigsaw groups, we had to be sure that the experimental conditions were different. First, the control classes really had to be "teacher-oriented" rather than "student-oriented." While all of the control classes were normally taught in a teacher-oriented, competitive manner, we specifically asked the control teachers to agree not to break their class into small groups, and especially not into cooperative ones, during the course of the research.

Second, we needed to ensure that the jigsaw technique was used similarly in all jigsaw classes. To achieve this, we conducted a series of workshops to provide teachers with identical training in using the jigsaw method so that we could be fairly sure that they were conducting their classes in as much the same way as possible. Teachers in our control classes did not attend these workshops. Therefore, if there were any differences between the two types of classes in students' attitudes or liking for one another, we could conclude that these differences were due to the effect of the jigsaw groups. Without such certainty about what was happening in the jigsaw classes, though, we could not be sure that differences in attitude change or liking could be attributed solely to the jigsaw method.

The workshop we eventually developed is described in some detail in Appendix D. In the first workshop, which lasted five days and was held just before school began, the teachers learned how to use the jigsaw method by experiencing it themselves. They learned skills to help the jigsaw groups function smoothly, and came to view their role in the jigsaw method as one of being group facilitators rather than of being the primary providers of information. In addition, teachers adapted their own curriculum material to the jigsaw method and devised strategies to help students with specific learning or behavior problems that might develop in their groups. Several half-day workshops were held during the following months to provide additional training and to allow teachers to interact with and help one another.

Back in the classroom, the jigsaw teachers were asked to assign their students to small groups that were as heterogeneous as possible; it mattered very much to us that each group consist of as wide a range of students as possible. Some of the reasons for this have been discussed previously. An additional reason has to do with the efficacy of the research: we wanted to be sure that our data would apply to all students. For example, if many groups had consisted of only boys, our data would have been limited primarily to groups consisting of all boys. In other words, the generalizability of our data, the extent to which it would apply to typical groups in most classrooms, would have been severely restricted, and we would not have learned very much about the effect of jigsaw groups as they would be used in most classrooms. Accordingly, we asked teachers to distribute differences in ethnicity, academic ability, and sex as evenly as possible among groups. In addition, students who were either close friends or bitter enemies were not placed together. Groups usually consisted of five to six members and generally met for forty to forty-five minutes a day, at least three days a week.

Of course, simply putting students in the same small group was no guarantee that they would be able to work together effectively from the very beginning. In fact, from what we know about children that age, there is every indication to the contrary. To facilitate the transition to jigsaw learning, teachers led their groups in a series of teambuilding exercises before the students actually began to teach one another. The short exercises were designed to make it easier for the students to teach as well as to improve their listening and helping skills.

For example, in order to help students learn the importance of listening to one another, we designed an exercise in which they introduced themselves by name—all at the same time! Of course, no one heard anyone else's name since they had all been talking at once. In this simple exercise, the merits of taking turns and listening to one another were immediately obvious to the students. After the laughter subsided, students in each group would discuss not being able to listen while they were talking, thereby setting the scene for group agreement that listening would be a very important part of teaching and learning.

In another exercise, students in each group drew a group picture by passing the pen from person to person. Each time a student had the pen he added something to the picture. After several rounds of pen-passing, a finished picture emerged—one to which each person had made a contribution. The discussion after the group-picture exercise invariably focused upon the importance of each member's contribution. Students spontaneously expressed their belief that the group's work would be incomplete without everyone's full participation and that one person trying to dominate the activities necessarily resulted in one or more persons feeling left out. Thus the group picture, fun and quick as it was, became a convenient vehicle for illustrating that working together rather than separately sometimes can be very useful.

Each of the teambuilding exercises was short. The exercises as a whole provided students with experiences to help them focus upon skills that would be important to their success as teachers and learners in jigsaw groups. As you recall, these exercises were used only at the beginning of the groups, before actual teaching began, as a way to lay the foundation for effective group functioning.

In order to reinforce these skills and help the students improve their group's functioning, the last five minutes of each group period were set aside for group processing. During this time, students used guidelines developed during teambuilding to assess how well their group had functioned that day. These guidelines focused on the kinds of things group members might do in order to help one another teach and learn more effectively. Each student would fill out a checklist including such items as whether people in their group listened to one another, whether they asked each other questions to facilitate teaching, whether they looked at one another, whether they took turns talking, and so on. After filling out checklists for individual members as well as for the group as a whole, groupmates would discuss their checklists, pinpoint their trouble areas, and reach decisions on what they would try to do differently next time.

The teacher moved from group to group during this processing in order to demonstrate ways to give noncritical, constructive feedback about how an individual or the group as a whole was behaving. The goal of all this was to increase the students' awareness of how they could improve their functioning as a learning group.

We have already described a typical jigsaw session. Here is a brief overview. Each group member was responsible for learning all the curriculum material, but each student had direct access to only his part of the material—the part he was to teach to others. Since he had to depend on his groupmates to teach him the rest of the material, each student learned that it was essential for all of his groupmates to do a good job of teaching their parts of the material. Along with that, students had to do a good job of listening. And, if material being taught was not clear, groupmates had to learn to ask the student teacher to clarify the material. Moreover, it was functional to learn to ask in ways that would help the student do a better job of teaching rather than to be destructive or intimidating. In essence, the students in each group were putting their knowledge together a piece at a time, each student contributing his piece of the jigsaw puzzle of material.

THE RESULTS

All the detailed planning described in the previous section was done so that we could accurately evaluate the effectiveness of the jigsaw method. Let's take a detailed look at our results.

THE LIKING MEASURE

This measure was used to find out how much students liked one another and what effect, if any, the jigsaw groups had upon this liking. As already described, the measure consisted of ratings, from seven to one, that each student gave to every other student in the class. Of special concern to us was how the jigsaw experience affected the students within each group. We predicted that their liking for one another would increase. In addition, we were interested in how well the students liked people who were not in their group.

Before we examine the results, let us take a closer look at this hypothesis. Imagine a situation where all five members of a group have grown to like one another very well during their six weeks of learning together. But further suppose that these five students had become such a tight-knit group that they no longer studied or played much with other classmates as they had done before the groups. Worse still, suppose that these five buddies actually came to dislike the other students. In such a situation the jigsaw groups would clearly have had an impact, but it would not be entirely beneficial, to say the least. In order to ascertain whether or not this was happening, we calculated two types of liking scores for each student in the jigsaw classes. One represented the average of the liking ratings the student gave her groupmates, and the other represented the average of the liking ratings given to all other classmates.

Comparing these two scores for each student, we found that students did grow to like their groupmates more than their other classmates, even though the students had liked their group-mates slightly *less* than their other classmates at the beginning of the study. Moreover, this increased liking for groupmates did *not* occur at the expense of the others, because liking for others also increased, although it did not increase nearly as much as the liking for groupmates. In short, *by the end of the study, the students liked both groupmates and other classmates better than when the study began.* Thus, the jigsaw has a generally favorable effect on the liking of students for each other throughout the class—especially within each working group.

THE ATTITUDE QUESTIONNAIRE

Our second instrument, the attitude questionnaire, allowed us to determine the differences in attitudes between students in the jigsaw classes and students in the control classes. As you remember, in order to measure attitudes, we asked students in both types of classes to complete a 22-item questionnaire twice—at the beginning and at the end of the six-week research period. The attitudes covered such dimensions as liking for school, self-esteem, and competitiveness. For each dimension we compared the answers given by students in the jigsaw classes with the answers given by students in the control classes. The results follow.

Liking for School

Casual observation suggests that in traditional teacher-oriented classrooms, boredom grows as time goes on. As boredom grows, dissatisfaction grows. What happens in jigsaw classrooms? We hypothesized that students in the jigsaw classes would like school better (over time) than students in the control classes. To test this hypothesis, we combined the answers to these questions: "How much do you like school this year?," "When you are in the classroom, how happy do you feel?," and "When you are in the classroom, how bored do you feel?"

At the end of six weeks, students in the control classes liked school less than they had at the beginning. Students in the jigsaw classes, however, liked school as well as they had at the beginning. This confirmed our hypothesis: jigsaw groups do help students sustain interest in school, thus combatting the declining interest that we found in teacher-oriented classes.

Since students in our study were from several ethnic groups, it is reasonable to assume that they might have had somewhat different answers to the same questions. For that reason, we looked at each ethnic group separately. In fact, Anglos, blacks, and Mexican-Americans did differ in their answers to the questions about liking school. Anglos in the jigsaw groups grew to like school more during the six weeks while Anglos in the control classes liked school less. So, for Anglos, the jigsaw groups actually caused an increase in liking for school. In contrast, the black students in the jigsaw groups liked school slightly less, but they still liked school more than the blacks in the control classes did. Thus, for black students, the jigsaw groups succeeded in reducing a tendency to lose interest in school. Results for the Mexican-American students were quite different and surprising. The Mexican-Americans in the control classes showed an increase in liking for school that was greater than the increase in liking for school in the jigsaw classes.

To what can we attribute this unexpected finding for the Mexican-American students? We feel that the most likely explanation for these differences is traceable to the language problems (and the accompanying embarrassment) frequently encountered by Mexican-American students. In traditional classrooms, Mexican-Americans often learn how to keep quiet, and the longer they are in the classroom the more comfortable they may become with this state of affairs. Along comes the jigsaw technique, which forces them to undergo the discomfort of speaking English. This may have caused them to like school less over the six-week testing period. But if this speculation is true, we would expect their liking for school to increase after prolonged exposure to the jigsaw—that is, after they become accustomed to speaking more in school. Or, in a similar vein, if Mexican-American students were in a situation where they would not feel embarrassed by any difficulty with language— for example, if they were in the majority in the classroom— they would not be susceptible to discomfort in the jigsaw situation. In his Ph.D. dissertation, Robert Geffner, one of the students assisting us, tested this proposition by conducting the same experiment in classrooms in Watsonville, California, where Mexican-Americans are in the majority. In general Geffner replicated our findings, and in addition showed that, in this situation, Mexican-American children tended to like school better in the jigsaw situation than in competitive classrooms.

Overall, the results are very positive, showing that students in the jigsaw classes grew to like school more than students in control classes. We also learned of these positive effects in other, more casual ways. Both students and teachers involved in the jigsaw groups informally commented on the fun that students had in the groups. They enjoyed the freedom to "behave," to interact with their classmates, and to move around more freely than in a traditional classroom. In addition, the students expressed satisfaction with their involvement in their own learning, which was an important part of the group experience.

Self-esteem

A person's self-concept generally consists of all the attitudes, abilities, and assumptions he holds concerning himself which act as a guide for behavior. Self-esteem is the evaluative component of the self-concept. One can define self-esteem as the amount of worthiness and power that an individual perceives in himself. Where does one find evidence about one's own worthiness and power? A major source of self-worth and power is the result of interpersonal interactions with relevant others, such as family members, teachers, and friends. David Franks and Joseph Marolla have termed this "outer self-esteem." Another source of self-esteem ("inner self-esteem") is a function of real accomplishment: success or failure in a person's interaction with the environment. A moment's reflection will show how both of these factors can be enormously important in the classroom.

In education, these two dimensions of self-esteem develop from a child's interpretation of the feedback from teachers and classmates as well as from his own learning experiences. According to researchers such as Fritz Heider and E. E. Jones, individuals have a tendency to go beyond the available information in order to try to explain the causes of someone's behavior—even their own. In general, when viewing her own behavior, an individual will explain her successes by personal attributions (i.e., "Success was due to my ability"), and resort to situational attributions in trying to explain her failures (i.e., "My failure was due to feeling sick that day"). Thus, our self-attributions generally protect our self-esteem. In the classroom, then, a student would probably attribute a good performance to his personal ability, knowledge, intelligence, etc., which would enhance his inner self-esteem. Indeed, M. V. Covington and Richard Beery report that success-oriented students generally make personal attributions when they perform well and usually attribute failure to a lack of effort. In addition, there is substantial evidence that students with high self-esteem generally have high achievement levels in school. In summaries of the research in this field, Covington, Beery, and William Purkey suggest that high self-esteem leads to better achievement, and conversely that high performance leads to a high self-esteem. It appears that positive experiences, personal attributions, higher expectations, and anticipated success are all involved in self-fulfilling prophecies which lead to improved self-esteem and subsequently to higher achievement levels in school.

What happens when a child experiences failure? Covington and Beery state that the lack of successful experiences and the scarcity of rewards in the classroom can lead some students to learn to expect failure. These students give up and stop trying to succeed: low self-esteem and low achievement are maintained through negative self-fulfilling prophecies. In these cases, it appears that the students make situational attributions (e.g., luck) for the few successes they might have, and personal attributions for their failures (e.g., poor ability and low self-worth). These same types of attributions are often made by classmates and even by some teachers with regard to those students who are failing in school. Thus, the interactions among students can also lead to these self-defeating self-fulfilling prophecies. Clearly, competitiveness exacerbates this process.

It is sometimes assumed that working cooperatively blunts individuality and therefore makes people feel less important as individuals. Just as we did not want to enhance student liking by creating cohesive but antagonistic teams, neither did we want to foster group interdependence at the expense of individual feelings of self-esteem. It is our contention that the reverse happens: that people who work together receive encouragement and positive feedback from their co-workers more often than not—because of the interdependence of the situation. Moreover, in the process of working together individuals learn to trust their own effectiveness. The combination of these two processes should lead to an increase in self-esteem. We felt that this would be particularly true in our situation because of the fact that a child's performance on tests is his own. That is, while children *learn* cooperatively, their scores on exams are not an average of the group score, but rather are a reflection of each individual's mastery of the material.

We tested this hypothesis by combining the results of three questions: "How much do you like being yourself?," "When you are in the classroom, how important do you feel?," and "When you are in class, how often do you feel you can learn whatever you try to learn?" As before, the answers given by students in jigsaw classes were compared to the answers of students in control classes.

As we suspected, this comparison showed that, during the six-week period, *students in the jigsaw classes increased in self-esteem to a greater extent than students in competitive classes.* Apparently, giving students the opportunity to participate in

teaching as well as in learning made students feel like an important part of the learning process, and thus worthy individuals.
In competitive classrooms, such as our control classes, students
are primarily recipients rather than givers of information, a
situation which apparently does little to involve students actively in the learning process or to enhance their positive feelings about themselves. As the story told by one of our teachers
earlier in this chapter indicates, Paul was no longer seen as
dumb by his classmates. Being valued by the people you are
working with is an important step toward higher self-esteem.

Competition

Does the jigsaw experience change students' attitudes toward
competing and winning at all costs? We hypothesized that compared to students in the competitive classes, students in the
jigsaw classes would have a decreased preference for competitive behaviors. This hypothesis was tested by the questionnaire
item, "I would rather beat a classmate than help him." The
answers indicate that students in the jigsaw classes grew less
competitive over the six weeks while students in the control
classes grew more competitive.

This lowered competitiveness seemed to extend beyond the
classroom groups as well. As mentioned at the beginning of this
chapter, jigsaw teachers reported that teachers not involved in
our study but teaching the students at some time each week
(e.g., music or physical education teachers) remarked about the
improved attitudes and behavior of the jigsaw students. It seems
that classroom exposure to cooperation produced a lessening
of unproductive competitiveness in related settings as well as in
the classroom.

Learning from Others

Another important aspect of our results concerns the students' views of their experience, whether or not they felt other
students could be a source of learning for them. We hypothesized that students in jigsaw classes would come to believe that
they could learn from other students. The question "Can you

learn anything from other kids in your class?" was the test for this hypothesis. We found that, over the six weeks, students in the jigsaw classes increasingly believed they could learn from other students. Conversely, students in the control classes decreased in this belief. The experience of teaching and being taught by classmates was clearly a successful one for the students in the jigsaw groups: they did learn to use their peers as resources. The results of this hypothesis provide an exciting kind of support for our enthusiasm about the jigsaw groups: the students who participate in this method of teaching report that it works.

PERFORMANCE IN THE JIGSAW CLASSROOM

We have shown that the jigsaw groups have many benefits for students, but we have presented no data on their academic performance in relation to students in more typical classrooms. You might be wondering if students who have such a good time talking in their jigsaw groups actually learn very much, and so did we. No matter how much happiness and self-confidence a teaching technique provides, it is of dubious benefit to the students if it interferes with their mastery of the subject matter.

Previous research conducted by other investigators suggested that academic performance would be at least as high with the jigsaw as it is with more typical classroom techniques. For example, such research shows that both pupils and tutors achieve academic gains following peer tutoring. Also, this research shows that cooperation in general is associated with high academic performance.

In order to investigate this question, we needed to conduct a separate study. Precise data on exam performance from our six-week classroom experiments would have been impossible to gather because of the problems involved in coordinating such a large number of classrooms and in requiring teachers to teach the same material and give identical exams over a long period of time. We simply lacked the power to coordinate such an experiment. Accordingly, together with our colleagues Bill Lucker and David Rosenfield, we designed a short-term study to measure the effects of the jigsaw technique on academic performance. Our study lasted two weeks and involved about 300 fifth- and sixth-grade students from five elementary schools in Austin, Texas. Six jigsaw teachers and five teachers using competitive classroom approaches participated in the study. The latter teachers were highly competent and respected; their classes had approximately the same ethnic composition and reading skills as the jigsaw classes. The curriculum consisted of a unit on colonial America taken from a fifth-grade textbook, plus supplementary materials. For the jigsaw classes, the curriculum content was partitioned for jigsaw presentation, but otherwise it was identical to that used in the competitive classes.

Before the unit was introduced, we conducted a pre-test of the materials on colonial America. After the unit was completed, we administered a post-test. The data show that before the unit was begun there was no difference in knowledge about colonial America between students in jigsaw and competitive classes. However, after the unit was completed, students in the jigsaw groups scored considerably higher on the post-test than students in competitive classes. Looking at the test scores by ethnic groups, it was clear that the difference in performance between jigsaw and competitive classes was primarily due to the scores of the minority students. Specifically, the data show that in integrated schools Anglos learned equally well in both jigsaw and competitive classes, but blacks and Mexican-Americans learned *much more* in jigsaw than in competitive classes.

Why should minority students benefit academically from jigsaw groups more than Anglo students do? Researchers working in other cities have shown that many Anglo students seem better prepared than minority students to compete successfully in school. If this is the case in Austin, it may be that some of the minorities gain by working closely with Anglos in jigsaw groups. For example, some minority students may benefit from increased use of English; others may profit from the informal tutoring among friends that the structure of the jigsaw groups promotes. Other minorities may become excited by school work for the first time as a result of their increased freedom of expression and the intensive peer interaction within the groups or by the group's license to make decisions about choice and manner of exploring the subject matter. Note, however, that there is no support for the idea that high-achieving students suffer in jigsaw classes even though low-achieving students improve; rather, our data show that in jigsaw groups some students improve markedly while others perform at a characteristically high level. This is a very important aspect of our technique: *the low-achieving children benefit from the high-achieving children; the high-achieving children are not hampered by the low-achieving ones.* We are convinced that the reason high-achieving students are not hampered lies primarily in two integral features of the jigsaw method:

(1) The high-achieving students are specifically encouraged to enjoy the new role of teacher. That is, while the low-achieving students are taking the time to learn the material, the high-achieving students do not simply sit around, yawn, look out the window, and become frustrated, but are challenged to do a good job of teaching.

(2) The exams are a function of an individual's performance. High achievers are not penalized by others' lower grades. No matter how much improvement a low-achieving child experiences, it is unlikely that she will surpass or equal the performance of a child who has been highly successful academically for several years. Moreover, no matter how much experience a highly successful child has in cooperative learning, she still enjoys doing well and expects to be rewarded equitably for a good performance. Thus, if the scores of group members were averaged, the high-achieving students would undoubtedly experience frustration at receiving a grade that is somewhat lower than her merit. In the jigsaw method, this does not happen.

COOPERATION AND EMPATHY

Why does cooperative interaction enhance pro-social behavior in the classroom? It is our belief that one of the crucial mechanisms underlying the effects of cooperative behavior on liking, positive attributions, self-esteem, and performance is *empathy*. Our reasoning is based in part upon Jean Piaget's analysis. According to Piaget's theory, children learn and develop by interacting with their environment. Through the active process of resolving social and cognitive conflicts, children construct their ways of viewing the world. If they engage in a cooperative rather than a competitive process, it seems likely that the nature of their interaction should increase their abilities to take one another's perspective.

This hypothesis was recently put to the test by one of our students, Diane Bridgeman, in her Ph.D. dissertation. Specifically, she assessed the relationship between cooperative learning and role-taking abilities with 120 fifth-grade students from three Santa Cruz County elementary schools. A revised version of M. J. Chandler's role-taking cartoon series was used to assess the students' perspective-taking abilities. Each of the cartoons depicts a central character caught up in a chain of psychological cause-and-effect events, so that the character's subsequent behavior is shaped by, and fully comprehensive only in terms of, the events that have already happened. In one of the sequences, for example, a boy who had been saddened by seeing his father off at the airport began to cry when he later received a gift of a toy airplane similar to the one which had carried his father away. Midway in each sequence, a second character is introduced in the role of a late-arriving bystander who witnesses the resultant behaviors of the principal character, but is not privy to the antecedent events which brought them about. It is possible to place the subject in a privileged position in relation to the story character whose role the subject is later asked to assume. The degree to which the subject is able to set aside facts known only to himself and adopt a perspective measurably different from his own can then be determined.

Students in the cooperative classrooms were better able to put themselves in the bystander's place; students in the control classroom made significantly more egocentric statements on behalf of the role of the bystander. For example, when the mailman delivered the toy airplane to the little boy, students in competitive classrooms tended to assume that the mailman knew the boy would cry; that is, they believed that the mailman knew that the boy's father had recently left town on an airplane simply because they (the subjects) were privy to this information. On the other hand, students who had participated in a jigsaw group were much more successful at taking the mailman's role, realizing that the mailman could not possibly have predicted that the boy would cry upon receiving a toy airplane.

The role-taking tasks were administered to all students before and after eight weeks of classroom learning. The cooperative, interdependent classes constituted the experimental condition and the more competitive, teacher-centered classes constituted the control condition.

The results from this study are consistent with both Piaget's assumptions and the assumptions underlying the cooperative process. Both role-taking of rational thought (considering the logical perspective of another) and role-taking of affective thought (considering the emotional perspective of another) showed a significant increase after the cooperative experience. There was no change in the role-taking abilities of the students in the control classrooms who were taught in more competitive ways. Thus, in addition to clarifying the social developmental importance of cooperative learning, the results of this experiment demonstrate that the positive effects of the jigsaw experience can transfer from a classroom setting to a nonclassroom setting.

SUMMARY OF MAJOR RESULTS

To summarize the major results from the experiments described in this chapter: students in jigsaw classrooms increased their liking for their groupmates without decreasing their liking for other people in their classroom; students in jigsaw classrooms tended to increase their liking for school to a greater extent than children in nonjigsaw classrooms; children in jigsaw classrooms increased in self-esteem, decreased in competitiveness, and viewed their classmates as learning resources in relation to students in nonjigsaw classrooms. Black and Mexican-American students in jigsaw classrooms learned the material significantly better than black and Mexican-American students in nonjigsaw classrooms (as measured by objective test results). Anglo students performed as well in the jigsaw groups as in the nonjigsaw groups. Finally, children in jigsaw classrooms (compared to children in competitive classrooms) showed a greater ability to put themselves in the role of another person, even outside of the school environment. Taken together, these results show a strong, positive pattern of behaviors, feelings, and abilities which can be attributed to jigsaw groups.

The essential aspects of our early research have been replicated successfully in various parts of the country. Perhaps the most extensive systematic replication is Robert Geffner's Ph.D. dissertation in the public schools of Watsonville, California. Geffner conducted a highly sophisticated experiment in which he demonstrated the superiority of jigsaw groups to competitive groups on several pro-social behaviors. Moreover, he showed that cooperative learning was more effective when compared with children being taught in other innovative small groups. Thus what is important in producing the pro-social behavior we have described is neither innovation per se nor small group per se; rather, the essential ingredient is cooperation. Several other researchers have attained results similar to ours, including David Johnson and his colleagues in school systems in Minnesota, and Stuart Cook and his associates in Colorado.

NOTES

1. For more detailed reporting of our research data, see the articles by Aronson et al., 1975; Blaney et al., 1977; and Lucker et al., 1977, cited in the reference section.

2. For a discussion of cooperative athletic games, see *Every Kid Can Win* by Terry Orlick and Cal Botterill (Nelson-Hall, 1975).

Cooperation as One Part of the Classroom Experience 8

*P*icture the following scene: Two ten-year-old children are facing each other across a table, playing a game. In each child's hand is a string connected to a plastic block which holds a small round marble in a hole. The marble holder can be moved in either direction, depending on which string is pulled. At first glance, the game bears a superficial resemblance to tug-o'-war, with the object being to pull the plastic holder toward oneself so that the marble will drop into a goal on either end of the table. But as the children soon learn, the game differs from tug-o'-war in one crucial way: the marble holder is constructed in such a way that if both players were to pull hard, it would break apart—and neither player could succeed in pulling the marble to his goal. That is, in order for one child to achieve his goal, the other child would need to relax his string. Each child was informed that for each marble he succeeded in pulling to his goal, he would receive a prize. The prizes were very attractive to the children. Clearly, the sensible strategy would be some form of turn taking. In that way, each child would attain a prize on 50 percent of the trials.

This game is an example of the kind of game-playing situation utilized in a series of experiments performed by Millard Madsen, Spencer Kagan, and Linden Nelson. How do white American children perform in this kind of game? Dismally. In this and similar games they tend to behave in "irrationally competitive" ways—for example, pulling hard and breaking the marble holder apart on trial after trial—so that neither player ends up with many prizes. In this kind of game the behavior of Anglo children is in sharp contrast to that of children from other cultural backgrounds, such as Mexicans, Mexican-Americans, black Americans, and Israelis raised on a kibbutz, who have no difficulty in developing a cooperative, turn-taking mode of playing. These results indicate either that Anglo children, in the main, have not mastered the skill of cooperation or that they fail to recognize a situation where cooperation is in their own best interest. The major goal of jigsaw learning is to help children learn cooperation as a skill and to sensitize children to situations which require that skill.

And it works. If you, the reader, have stayed with us this long, no doubt you have gotten the impression that we are enthusiastic about the jigsaw technique. It's true. We believe that the jigsaw has developed into a practical method of learning that produces great benefits—both intellectual and emotional—at little or no cost. The research bears us out: time and time again, under controlled scientific conditions, the jigsaw technique has shown itself superior to more competitive modes of learning on a variety of measures, including self-esteem, liking for school, and performance on exams. Virtually all of the teachers who have tried it have been pleased, not only with its impact upon their students but with the new role and behaviors that they (the teachers) have assumed in the classrooms. But it would be dysfunctional if, in our enthusiasm, we went overboard and created the impression that the jigsaw technique is the one and only method that should be used in the classroom. We don't believe this to be true. No single approach to classroom learning is perfect. There are some serious limitations in the jigsaw approach that make it imperative that it be used in conjunction with other methods. In Chapter 6, we looked at some specific problems (e.g., the poor reader, the "trouble maker") and offered some suggested solutions. But in addition to those there are some general limitations for which there may not be ready solutions.

THE SUBJECT MATTER

One limitation involves the subject matter. Throughout this book, our examples have all been drawn from the area of social studies, which includes history, geography, civics, etc. Our sample jigsaw curriculum (see Appendix B) is, likewise, a social studies lesson. There is a reason for this: the easiest subject matter to work with in jigsaw groups is narrative material where the major skills involved are reading and comprehension. This does not mean that other subjects cannot be taught, only that it is usually more difficult to fit them into the jigsaw format.

Our general rule of thumb is that a teacher probably should not try to apply the jigsaw technique to material that is *conceptually novel*, by which we mean curriculum material that requires students to utilize a skill they haven't learned yet. Just as we would not attempt to assign *The Life of Joseph Pulitzer* to a group of six children who didn't know how to read, by the same token we would not assign "subtraction" to a group of students who had not yet tasted the joys and rigors of solving mathematical problems. This is not to say that the jigsaw method is inappropriate for math. We know of several teachers who have successfully employed the jigsaw method for the instruction of math, language arts, biology, and other subjects clearly outside the realm of social studies. But in these areas the jigsaw has been used primarily to *review* material previously taught by more traditional methods.

Another limitation involving subject matter has to do with a reading assignment which is *cumulatively interwoven,* by which we mean that because of the nature of the material it would be difficult to understand part three without having first read and understood parts one and two. Thus while it is easy to grasp Joseph Pulitzer's middle years without knowing about his childhood and young adulthood, it would be far more difficult to make much sense out of Chapter 3 of a detective story without having first read Chapters 1 and 2. Accordingly, if you were a fifth-grader and you were assigned part three of a story or subject matter that is, by its very nature, cumulatively interwoven, chances are you would not be able to grasp its meaning sufficiently well to communicate it meaningfully to members of your jigsaw group. In situations like these, teachers have either employed more traditional techniques or have allowed all students an initial quick reading of the entire assignment, followed by a deeper, more elaborate review using the jigsaw technique.

GRADE LEVEL OF STUDENTS

Thus far, systematic research evaluating the jigsaw technique has been performed only on fifth- and sixth-grade students. In addition, several fourth-grade teachers have tried the technique and report successful experiences. On the early end of the spectrum we have found that young children—even kindergartners—are perfectly able and willing to engage in cooperative behavior. Nonetheless, our attempts to institute the jigsaw technique prior to the fourth grade have not been easy. There are two major problems. First, virtually all of the students in a group need at least a minimal proficiency in reading for the jigsaw to work, and one cannot count on this general proficiency in the first few grades of elementary school. Second, the understanding of the basic elements of jigsawing requires a certain degree of conceptual ability. While we've found that most six-year-olds can eventually grasp what is required, it often necessitates a longer period of time to thoroughly acquaint them with the system than is the case for youngsters ten years old and above.

At the upper end of the classroom continuum, there seems to be no limit. High school and middle school teachers have utilized the jigsaw with great success. Moreover, some of our colleagues have put it into operation at the university level, even with highly technical material like collections of research reports in the psychology of perception and social psychology. At the university level the students were placed in jigsaw groups and met on their own time outside of class. The only intervention made by the instructor consisted of a brief training session designed to spell out the degree of specificity required in the actual reporting so that a semblance of uniformity could be achieved. That is, in technical reporting it is conceivable that if the students are not instructed, some reports might be overly detailed and others might be too sparse. A brief instruction about the appropriate degree of complexity proved to be invaluable. Virtually all of the university students who utilized the jigsaw opportunities reported good results: mastery of the material in far less time than if they would have read it on their own, plus the added enjoyment of companionship and the intellectual stimulation brought about by the sharing of a variety of perspectives.

BOREDOM AND THE BRIGHT STUDENT

We are frequently asked what happens to the brightest students in the jigsaw situation. Don't they become impatient, bored, or resentful of the slower students? Boredom is not uncommon in elementary school regardless of the techniques being used, and it would be grossly misleading for us to imply that children working with the jigsaw process were never bored or impatient. While today's teacher is better trained than her earlier counterpart, she must also contend with the higher expectancies and lower thresholds for boredom extant among most young children, due in part to the ubiquitous presence of TV. No matter how gifted the teacher, how exciting the subject matter, how engrossing the educational technique, the chances are that for most elementary school children the classroom lacks the excitement, entertainment value, movement, and the sheer pleasure of *Sesame Street* or other related productions. Moreover, because their minds are so quick, bright students tend to be among the most easily bored if events are moving too slowly for them.

While it may be impossible to eliminate boredom from the school experience, teachers who have used the jigsaw technique report a great deal *less* boredom among their students than is the case in a more competitive classroom atmosphere. Our data support this observation: children in jigsaw classes do like school better than children in the control classes, and this is true for the bright students as well as the slower students. There is an old adage, *docemur docendo* (he who teaches learns). This is clearly the case in the jigsaw situation. Teaching can be an exciting change of pace for a student. It frees her from being a more or less passive receptacle of information and allows her the opportunity to try a new skill. Not only does this almost certainly reduce boredom, but if introduced properly it can also reduce the impatience that bright students otherwise experience when slower students are experiencing difficulty. By developing the mind set of "teacher" the bright students can turn what might have been a boring, mark-time, impatient experience into an exciting challenge. And, as previously reported, not only does this challenge produce psychological benefits, but the learning is frequently more thorough.

One other point is relevant in this context. In developing the jigsaw method we took special pains to minimize conflict and/or resentment among students. We dealt with this concern by developing a strategy that makes the jigsaw different from other forms of cooperation in an important way. Although children learn the material in a cooperative fashion in the jigsaw, they are tested individually and receive individual scores rather than an average of the group score. Thus a particularly bright student has the opportunity to shine individually; in no way can her score be diminished by the exam performance of a less gifted student. This aspect of the jigsaw has proven itself to be congenial with the desires of most students as well as those of their parents. Again, the data on this score are remarkable: in the school systems where we have worked, parents who have responded have tended to express a range of feelings from slight skepticism to great enthusiasm; serious parental complaint has been almost totally absent. We believe that the reason parents are pleased is partly that the slower children do not learn at the expense of the brighter ones or vice versa.

While the jigsaw has proven to be one good way to reduce boredom, there are other ways. Indeed, one surefire way any teacher can reduce boredom is to refuse to stick to one method, whether it is competitiveness, individually guided instruction, audiovisual presentations, or the jigsaw technique. Is the jigsaw compatible with these other methods? Let's take a long look.

FREQUENCY OF JIGSAWING

It may be particularly valuable to begin to answer that question by reiterating the fact that the jigsaw technique produces measurably beneficial effects, even when it forms only a small part of the child's day in school. Indeed, as we showed in Chapter 7, much of our research data compared competitive classrooms with competitive classrooms *in which the students participated in jigsaw groups for only three or four hours per week.*

The next question we might explore is whether or not there is a maximum. Casual observation of jigsaw classrooms indicates that the beneficial effects of cooperation become stronger as more time is spent in cooperative groups. Over the past several years, several teachers have utilized the jigsaw technique for a large part of each day. At least one teacher succeeded in adapting her curriculum material to the jigsaw technique to the point where children in her classes were spending approximately 80 percent of their class time in cooperative groups. She recently reported that the beneficial results were far clearer and more dramatic than when she was able to employ cooperative learning for only an hour or two per day. Of course, such data are not as rigorous as systematic experimental evidence; nonetheless, the reports of teachers on this score are so uniformly consistent that it seems reasonably safe to conclude that the kinds of positive effects of cooperation reported in this volume are a linear function of the amount of cooperation—that is, as jigsawing increases, so do the benefits.

But a few parents have raised the legitimate question that perhaps too much cooperation is dysfunctional in the long run. They argue that while the benefits of cooperation are clear, as long as our society is largely competitive we may be in danger of training children to cooperate so much that they may lose their ability to win in such competitive situations as gaining admission to college or medical school. We can readily understand this concern; competitiveness *is* pervasive in our society, and that's our point. It is so pervasive that a child could hardly avoid encountering competitive situations even if they were eliminated from the classroom altogether. Given the concern with winning that predominates in the society at large, it is our hunch that serious parental worry about children not learning how to compete is analogous to the obese person worrying about losing too much weight as a result of eliminating pastries from his diet. Nonetheless, it would be prudent, and we think beneficial, for students as well as for teachers, if the jigsaw technique were utilized as part of a variety of classroom strategies which might include individually guided instruction *as well as some competitive activities*. This may be especially necessary for some non-Anglo children, who may not have as much opportunity to learn competitive strategies in the family. This concern was articulated brilliantly in a recent paper by Antoine Garibaldi, an educational social psychologist. Garibaldi argues persuasively that as important as cooperation is, it might be a mistake to attempt to eliminate competition entirely from the educational process (even if it were possible). Part of Garibaldi's argument is frankly political: he feels that disadvantaged minorities must learn to compete so that they can begin to win their way into more fulfilling, rewarding, and powerful occupations. He further suggests that for many ethnic minorities the family does not provide the opportunity to learn to compete. We agree with his position. There is no way in which we would advocate the learning of the skill of cooperation at the expense of the learning of other skills—like, for example, the skill of *competing under appropriate conditions*.

And, as we have seen, there is no reason why cooperative and competitive techniques cannot co-exist in the same classroom. Indeed, recent research by David and Roger Johnson, Robert Slavin, and David DeVries—as well as our own research—demonstrates that both cooperation and competition can form part of the classroom process without a severe depletion of the benefits of cooperation. Recently a laboratory experiment by Cookie Stephan, James Kennedy, and Elliot Aronson has yielded results indicating that competition is less likely to produce harmful effects when it is preceded by the kinds of classroom behaviors that lead to friendly relations among the students. Before we describe that experiment, it might be helpful to sketch in the background. In earlier work, it had been demonstrated that, in general, people give themselves the benefit of the doubt when trying to attribute causes of their own success or failure. That is, when a person succeeds she tends to take personal credit ("It is because I am smart or skillful"); however, when she fails she does not attribute failure to a personal cause but to something about the situation ("The sun got in my eyes," "The exam was unfair," etc.). When the individual observes her competitor's behavior, it is a rather different story. In general, the other person is not given the benefit of the doubt. Quite the contrary; when the other person fails, the observer tends to make a personal attribution ("She's stupid," or "She doesn't know the material"). When her competitor succeeds, the observer tends to attribute the reason to the situation ("It was just a matter of luck"). Clearly, all of this behavior is protective of the individual's ego.

In the experiment by Stephan, Kennedy, and Aronson, it was shown that when competing against a *friend,* children will behave very gently toward her. Specifically, in this experiment, sixth-grade students played a game which involved throwing bean bags at a target. The experimenters arranged the situation so that some students succeeded while others failed. The students were placed in either a cooperative situation or a competitive situation. What is most interesting about their results is that when the children *beat a friend* in a competitive situation they did not lord it over her, but attributed their success to luck. These results suggest strongly that once friendship and empathy have been established, competition appears not to produce the kind of one-upmanship that can be demoralizing for the loser and harmful to the relationship between the winner and the loser. Based on these research data, we would suggest that competitiveness *not* be introduced into the classroom situation until friendships have begun to form as a result of cooperative strategies. Our guess is that this would be particularly important in situations like those in newly desegrated schools where, as we have seen, early competitiveness can exercise a particularly destructive impact on the self-esteem and performance of children from ethnic minorities and the interpersonal relations of children across ethnic lines.

THE ULTIMATE GOAL OF JIGSAW LEARNING

As we have said over and over again, our aim is not to train young people to be so cooperative that they will be out of place in a highly competitive society. Rather, our aim is to teach cooperation *as a skill* so that the individual can call on that skill under appropriate conditions—when cooperation is the most facilitative way to perform a task—even in an environment that is largely competitive. And it is quite clear that we have achieved some success: children we have worked with can and do cooperate under appropriate conditions. Moreover, children who have spent a year in a classroom where cooperation is the dominant mode of interaction apparently perform as well as they ever did, even a year later, when they have moved on to a classroom in which competition predominates. They haven't lost anything important. Our hope is that as a result of their jigsaw experience they have lost one thing: their tendency to compete, to try to beat the other person in situations where cooperation would be a more reasonable strategy.

Our hope goes even further: that children who have experienced the pleasures as well as the benefits of cooperation might even venture to attempt to cooperate in ambiguous situations. For most American children, reared as they are on a fairly steady diet of competitiveness, the strategy seems to be: when in doubt go out there and beat the other guy. Frankly, our ultimate goal is for children to begin to learn that cooperation is appropriate, functional, exciting, and humanizing in many more situations than they might have realized. It is even conceivable that as more and more children begin to experience some systematic cooperation as part of their educational experience, when they become adults the values of our society might begin to shift just a bit away from the relentless concern with winning. As we have seen, high standards and good performance are not necessarily incompatible with support, friendship, empathy, and a tolerance for individual differences.

Appendices

Appendices

APPENDIX A
TEACHER'S GUIDE TO THE MULTICULTURAL SOCIAL STUDIES CURRICULUM

FOREWORD TO MULTICULTURAL SOCIAL STUDIES UNIT

One of the first laws ever written in our national constitution concerned the right to be different. History has shown us that ever since the birth of our nation there has been one cultural group whose values have dominated across the land. Some educators refute this statement. They argue that the emergence of one cultural group is the result of a free-flowing, free mixing of cultures. They call America a melting pot of cultures.

The purpose of this curriculum is to present a more realistic picture of our nation's composite. Instead of viewing America as a melting pot, it can be seen as pluralistic—that is, being made up of many different social and ethnic groups that have contributed to the formation and maintenance of America. We designed a multicultural curriculum that recognizes cultural diversity as a fact of life in our society. By giving equal representation to cultural groups whose heritage, values, and identity have remained intact, it is our intention that the beauty of being different becomes clear. Once we recognize that there is no single model American, we can begin to learn freely from each other, learn about our heritage, and begin to understand who we are. In doing so, we will have a firmer idea where we are going and what we can contribute to this world. While the curriculum only touches on the history of California from a multicultural standpoint, a reoccurring emphasis is on individuality, uniqueness and cultural diversity.

CURRICULUM GUIDE

The following is a guide to the curriculum in Appendix A. Each unit is dealt with separately. A summary of the sections is given, activities that appear on cards are noted, and unit quizzes are included. The quizzes can simply be written on the board, although it is stressed that each student must take the quiz individually. (Cooperative learning is great, but the teacher and parents need to know how individuals are doing.) The quizzes are straightforward, short-answer questions geared to insure interdependence and learning of the material.

AUTHOR'S NOTE: Prepared by S. Radding and B. Davenport.

Some additional suggestions are:

(1) that the teacher supplement the curriculum with speakers from various minority groups;

(2) that the class participate in a culture day—the students can dress up in traditional clothing of another culture, make a traditional meal, etc.;

(3) that the class take field trips to cultural places and events;

(4) class projects such as making a mural or some other community-oriented project;

(5) films (good films can really add a lot to the curriculum);

(6) art projects such as making a collage, illustrating parts, etc.

MULTICULTURAL SOCIAL STUDIES FOR THE JIGSAW

UNIT A—INTRODUCTION

Section 1 (cards 1—5):[1]

Deals with the idea of cultural pluralism. It stresses the idea that people can live together yet keep many of their cultural ways.

Key concepts: culture
cultural pluralism
traditions

Section 2 (cards 6—10):

Brings in the idea of a melting-pot society. The advantages and disadvantages of this type of society are discussed.

Key concepts: dominance
melting-pot culture
culture shock

On-card Activity:

Discussion questions on key concepts.

Quiz:

Usually there will be only one quiz per unit. However, Unit A has a quiz after each section, to show the students a complete cycle of jigsawing. Many times they do not understand that cooperative learning does not

1. It is assumed that the teacher will put the entries in the sample curriculum (see Appendix B) on cards.

automatically mean "recess in class." If the marks are low on the first quiz, the teacher should go over the process again with the students. This first quiz should be used as an example. It is not hard, but one does need to pay attention in the group in order to learn the information and do well on the quiz. It takes a little time to get used to this new method of sharing and learning, and it should not be a threatening experience for anyone. A second end-of-the-unit quiz can serve as a second chance. Indeed, the teacher may want to disregard the grades on the first quiz.

Quiz, Unit A, Section 1:

(1) What are cultural traditions?

(2) What is culture?

(3) What is cultural pluralism?

(4) List five things that might be included in a culture.

(5) Must a culture give up its traditions in order to live peacefully with another culture? Explain.

Quiz, Unit A, Section 2:

(1) How do we learn about our culture and its traditions?

(2) Why do we often see our culture as the best way of life?

(3) What does the word "dominant" mean?

(4) What is the difference between cultural pluralism and a cultural melting pot?

UNIT B—AMERICAN INDIANS

Section 1 (cards 1—5):

Deals with the conflict between the new settlers and the Indians.

    Key concepts: tribe
                        missionaries
                        "civilized"

On-card Activity:

Hold a debate in your group. Two people take the role of the white settlers, two take the role of the Indians, and one person acts as the middleperson.

Section 2 (cards 6—10):

The new settlers begin to take over and the Indians are put on reservations. These new settlers thought that what they were doing was right. Unfortunately, it didn't work out so well for the Indians.

> Key concepts: immigrating
> treaties
> reservations
> survival

On-card Activity:

Discussion on "survival" and the things we need to survive.

Section 3 (cards 11—15):

Deals with the advantages and disadvantages of a melting-pot society. This section also looks at the Indian situation today.

> Key concepts: melting pot (again)
> economy
> relocation
> minority

On-card Activity:

Discussion of what could have been done and should be done to help the Indians.

Quiz, Unit B:

(1) What is a tribe?

(2) Why did the Spanish missionaries think that they lived a more civilized way of life?

(3) What happened to the Indians once the number of white men in the West started increasing?

(4) What does immigrating mean?

(5) What is a treaty?

(6) Why did the Indians have a hard time living on reservations?

(7) What does survival mean?

(8) Why did the White man want to keep the Indians on the reservations?

(9) What was the relocation program?

(10) What has happened to the American Indian of today?

UNIT C—MEXICANS

Section 1 (cards 1—5):

In the beginning the Mexicans and Anglo-Americans shared skills and land. Then conflict developed between them. Eventually a treaty was agreed upon that made it possible for the Mexicans to become citizens. This did not resolve the conflict.

> Key concepts: Anglo-American
> right
> citizen

On-card Activity:

Discussion of the conflict between Mexicans and Anglo-Americans.

Section 2 (cards 6—10):

Many Mexicans went back to their homeland. Others stayed, hoping to get their land back. Soon workers were needed for the mines and fields so the Mexicans were encouraged to come and work.

> Key concepts: banditos
> labor camps
> poverty

On-card Activity:

Discussion of how the jobs the Mexicans held kept them separated from the Anglo society.

Section 3 (cards 11—15):

Deals with the growth of Mexican-American migrant farmworkers, barrios, and the number of illegal aliens in California. Also included is a discussion of Cesar Chavez and his work for the United Farm Workers.

> Key concepts: migrant   aliens
> farmworkers   wetbacks
> prejudice   unions
> barrios

On-card Activity:

Discussion of the problems of life as a migrant farmworker.

Quiz, Unit C:

(1) What skills did the Mexicans teach the Anglo-Americans?

(2) What were some of the conditions in the treaty between Mexicans and the Anglo-Americans?

(3) What happened to the treaty?

(4) What did some of the Mexicans who remained in this country do?

(5) Why were the Mexicans encouraged to come to this land after 1865? Why did they want to come?

(6) What were labor camps?

(7) What is a migrant farmworker?

(8) What made life hard for Mexicans who were living in the cities?

(9) Why was a union formed by the farmworkers?

UNIT D—ASIANS

Section 1 (cards 1—5)—Chinese:

The Chinese first came to America seeking financial support for their families in China. Most of them lost their gold claims so they began work on the transcontinental railroad. Eventually many set up their own businesses in Chinatowns.

> Key concepts: Gold Rush
> gold claims
> transcontinental railroad
> Chinatowns

On-card Activity:

Discussion of cultural influence of Chinese on America.

Section 2 (cards 6—10)—Japanese:

One reason the Japanese came to this country was to avoid being drafted into their army. Many worked on the fields. Some even bought land. They shared their knowledge of working useless land into rich, fertile soil. When the United States and Japan were at war the Japanese living in the West were placed in camps.

> Key concepts: Americanization
> dignity

On-card Activity:

Discussion of the meaning of Americanization and the advantages and disadvantages of Americanization. Also, discussion of human dignity.

Quiz, Unit D:

(1) Why did the Chinese people come to America?

(2) Why did the Chinese people begin to work on the transcontinental railroad?

(3) What are Chinatowns?

(4) Why did the Japanese come to America?

(5) What skill did the Japanese people bring with them to America? Why was this important?

(6) What happened to the Japanese-Americans when Japan and the United States were at war?

UNIT E—BLACKS

Section 1 (cards 1—5):

The blacks were brought from Africa and sold as slaves. Eventually the North and South split on the issue of slavery. The Civil War brought the end of slavery.

> Key concepts: one's own free will
>   slave
>   abolitionists
>   Civil War

On-card Activity:

Discussion of what it would be like if the South had won.

Section 2 (cards 6—10):

The ending of slavery did not do much for the racial problems of the blacks. This section deals with the civil rights movement and the work of Dr. Martin Luther King, Jr.

> Key concepts: inferior race
>   civil rights movement
>   racial discrimination
>   law of the land
>   equal rights

On-card Activity:

Discussion on the problem of changing people's attitudes.

Section 3 (cards 11—15):

Deals with the struggles of the black people for equal rights and against the racism they have faced.

> Key concepts: employment opportunities
> busing
> racism
> reverse discrimination

On-card Activity:

Discussion of busing issue.

Quiz, Unit E:

(1) Why were the blacks brought to this country?

(2) How did the slaves live? How did they try to make their lives better?

(3) Who were the abolitionists and what did they do?

(4) What was the Civil War about?

(5) What does "inferior race" mean? How were the black people treated as an inferior race? List some examples of segregation.

(6) What was the civil rights movement about?

(7) What did the Civil Rights Act do?

(8) Why did kids get bused to other schools?

(9) What is discrimination?

UNIT F—CONCLUSION

Section 1 (cards 1—5):

Stevie Wonder's song "Black Man" is used as a take-off point to discuss the accomplishments of people of all races. The first card introduces the chorus of the song and the other cards each deal with separate races.

> Key concept: justice

On-card Activity:

Discussion of the contributions of all races to civilization.

Section 2 (cards 6—10):

The concept of stereotypes is presented with a hypothetical example of a boy who stereotypes all things that are red as being horrible. This section also deals with the idea of prejudice and how one gets that way. Unit ends with the idea that we all need to pull together in order to make this world a better place.

> Key concepts: stereotypes
> prejudice
> humankind

On-card Activity:

Discussion of differences between all people. Exercise in observation of their hands and the difference between them.

Quiz, Unit F:

(1) What is the main idea of Stevie Wonder's song "Black Man"?

(2) Name one contribution of each of the groups of people we have studied.

> American Indians
> Mexicans
> Whites
> Blacks
> Asians

(3) What is a stereotype? How does it affect one's view of people?

(4) How do we become prejudiced? How can we overcome our prejudices?

(5) What does it mean to be *free?*

APPENDIX B
SAMPLE CURRICULUM
Multicultural Social Studies

UNIT A—INTRODUCTION

A1. Our country is made up of many different groups of people. They all have helped make America the strong nation it is today. Who are these people? The groups we will be looking at are the Native Americans, Europeans, Asians, Africans, and South Americans.

A2. *Culture* is the way a group of people lives. In a single culture the people share the same rules, beliefs, attitudes, and style of living. For example, people of a certain culture may dress in the same way and eat the same kinds of food. What other things can you think of that would be included in a culture?

A3. When a country is made up of many separate cultures living side by side, it is called a land of *cultural pluralism.* In other words, cultural pluralism means that all these groups live and work together. However, they also practice their own cultural traditions.

A4. *Traditions* are the rules and beliefs that have been given to us by our parents. Traditions were given to our parents by their parents. Traditions are beliefs that have been handed down to us over the years. What traditions are practiced in your family?

A5. When different cultures live side by side, it is important that they understand each other's traditions. In this way they can work and live peacefully together. They can accept or learn from another culture's traditions without giving up their own.

A6. We learn about our culture and its traditions as we grow up. Many times we see our culture as the best way of life because it is the most comfortable for us. We understand it the best because it is the only way we know. We find it hard to understand why other people want to live in any other way.

AUTHOR'S NOTE: We wish to offer our appreciation to Saralee Radding and Barbara Davenport, who prepared this curriculum, and to Dr. Diane Bridgeman, who served as a consultant.

A7. The Anglo-American culture is the *dominant* culture in the United States. It has the most power and can influence other cultures to change their ways. For example, in the United States, children of all different cultures go to school where English is spoken. In many cases they must give up their own language in order to get along at school.

A8. When people give up their cultures in order to blend in the dominant culture, it is called a *melting pot.* When this happens, many cultural traditions are forgotten. How would you feel if you had to give up part of your culture? Discuss the difference between melting pot and pluralism.

A9. Those groups who have to change their way of life may experience *culture shock.* We will be looking at four of the many cultural groups in California's history. They are the Native Americans, Mexicans, Asians, and blacks. Each of these groups had to give up their way of life in order to adjust to the dominant culture.

A10. Throughout history all peoples have, at some time, had to give up some part of their cultural traditions. They did this in order to fit into the dominant culture. They experienced culture shock. At home tonight, trace your family background and find out what country(s) your family came from.

UNIT B—AMERICAN INDIANS

B1. Long before our European descendants came to America, there were millions of Indians living on this land. They make up many different tribes. A *tribe* is a group of people that live together and share a common culture. Indian tribes each had their own way of life. Some tribes hunted and fished for their food. Others gathered acorns and wild plants. Still others farmed.

B2. The Indian tribes practiced their own cultural traditions for many, many years. Then other groups of people started entering this country. They were seeking land, freedom, and riches. The first group who greatly affected the Indians' way of life was the Spanish *missionaries.* The Spanish, in hopes of obtaining the land, sent missionaries to teach the Indians their *civilized* way of life.

B3.   As history shows us, the white men and Indians have not gotten along well with each other. The white men were descendants of the first European settlers. They believed that they deserved the land for several reasons. They felt that because they were "civilized" they could make better use of the land. They also believed that since more of their people were entering the country, they needed room for them to live.

B4.   The Indians had many reasons for wanting to hold onto their land. They felt that the land was theirs to begin with. They also felt that the white man tricked and forced them into giving up their native land. Without their land, they could not keep their people together and hold onto their way of life.

B5.   Wars between the Indians and white men took place because each side thought that they had rights to the same land. As more and more white men began entering the country, the Indians became outnumbered. The Indians began losing their power to hold onto the land. Hold a debate in your group. Two people take the role of the white settlers, two people take the role of the Indians, and one person act as the middleperson.

B6.   During the early part of the 19th century, the country began to grow. Many people from all parts of Europe started *immigrating* to America. Soon more room was needed. These people began to move westward in search of land. Later, word spread that there was gold in California. The search for riches brought thousands of people westward.

B7.   The New Americans wanted to make this country both large and strong. Because the Indians were already on the land, they were seen as being in the way. These New Americans tried everything possible to make the land theirs. They tried to move the Indians to smaller areas of land. And when the Indians resisted, there was war!

B8.   *Treaties* were made between the white men and the Indians in order to keep peace. But as the desire for more land and wealth grew, the treaties were broken. The Indians were forced to move onto even smaller areas of land. These areas were governed by the white men and they were called reservations. Although the government said this land was Indian land, the Indians had difficulty practicing their own culture.

B9. The Indians were no longer the dominant culture. On *reservations* controlled by the United States government, the Indians were forced to practice the white man's way. They had to give up almost everything in their culture. But they had little help in learning the new way of life. The white men believed that they were helping the Indians. They gave them food, clothing, shelter, and what they believed was a better way of life.

B10. The Indians did not feel that they were being helped by the white men. Reservation life was hard. The Indians had a different cultural background, so it wasn't easy for them to take on a whole new way of life. Also, the Indians weren't taught necessary skills for survival in the white man's world. What do we mean when we say "survival"? What things do we need in order to survive?

B11. There were many reasons why the white men wanted to keep the Indians on reservations. One important reason was that many people in the government believed in the melting pot idea that we discussed earlier. They wanted all people living in this country to learn to live in the same way. What are the advantages or disadvantages of this?

B12. Although the Indians were expected to learn the white man's culture, they were not given the right to be citizens until 1924. Ten years later, a law was passed that allowed the Indians to practice their own way of life. But by this time, the Indians had become dependent on the American *economy.* Like everyone else, they needed to earn money in order to survive.

B13. In 1957, the government finally realized that the Indians needed jobs in order to live under good conditions. A program was set up to encourage Indians to move to the cities where jobs could be found. This was called the *relocation program.*

B14. City life for the Indians was hard. They got the worst jobs and lived in poor housing areas. These housing areas were called Indian ghettos. For many Indians, city life was just as hard as life on the reservation. For some, the culture shock was too much and they returned home. What do you think could have been done to help the Indians?

B15. Today the Indians are the poorest *minority* in America. Over half of them live on reservations under the worst conditions. Most families earn less than $3,000 a year. What do you think can be done to give equal opportunity to this important minority? Discuss.

UNIT C—MEXICANS

C1. As the Indians were being pushed further west by the New Americans, a new group of people was moving into what is now California. These were the Mexicans from the South. Like the New Americans, they too were seeking gold and riches.

C2. Soon the New Americans (called the Anglo-Americans) arrived. At first everything was peaceful. In fact, the Mexicans began to share their skills and knowledge about farming desert land. They showed them how to mine for gold and how to weave clothing.

C3. As more Anglo-Americans began moving westward, the two cultures came into conflict. War broke out and the Anglo-Americans won. Afterward they decided to sign a treaty. The treaty was an agreement between them to restore peace. This treaty said that all Mexicans living on U.S. land had the right to become *citizens* and to own the land. They also said that Spanish and English would be the two languages spoken in California.

C4. Soon the Anglo-American settlers believed that they were better and knew more than the Mexicans. They did not accept the Mexican culture. They didn't think the Mexicans deserved the land. They took it for themselves. This caused many problems for the Mexicans. For one thing, this meant that they had no place to raise their cattle because there was no place to put them.

C5. The Mexican people brought many valuable gifts to the new nation. Unfortunately the Anglo-Americans did not appreciate the Mexican-Americans. From the very beginning, the Anglo-Americans thought the Mexicans were lazy and unfriendly. The Anglo-Americans had difficulty accepting the values of another culture. To them, their way was the only way.

C6. Many Mexicans returned to their original homeland penniless. Others would not give up. They remained, trying to get their land back. But their struggle was useless. Frustrated, many formed gangs and raided new cities of the Anglo-Americans. The people of these gangs were called *banditos.*

C7.　During the beginning of the 1900s, the southwest was growing into a prosperous area. California had become a state by 1850. Towns and cities sprang up. Agriculture and mining became two of the main industries. As these industries grew, more workers were needed to maintain them.

C8.　At first slaves were used to work in the fields picking cotton. But slavery was outlawed in 1865. Orientals were used to pick crops as well as work on the railroads. But laws were passed that restricted the number of Orientals allowed in the country. As we can see, the minority groups worked the hardest jobs but the Anglos made the money.

C9.　Mexicans were encouraged to come to this new developed land. One reason they wanted to come was because their government was in a state of civil war. Many wanted to escape the *poverty* and unrest in their country. As soon as they arrived, they were put to work in mines, fields, and railroads.

C10.　While the Mexicans were working in these new industries, they lived in labor camps. Labor camps were cheap housing areas near the place of work. These labor camps separated the minority group physically, socially, and politically. In this way, they had little chance of participating in the main culture. Work was all they had time for. Discuss in detail how this would keep them separated from the Anglo society.

C11.　By the early 1900s large numbers of Mexicans began coming into the southwestern part of the United States. Most of them found jobs in Texas, Arizona, and California. Many worked in the fields as *migrant farmworkers.* This meant that they moved from place to place, depending on what crops were ready to be harvested. Can you see any problems with this type of life?

C12.　Most of the Mexican workers who came into the United States held on to their national heritage. However, their children did not. Being born in the United States made them natural citizens of America. This new generation were the Mexican-Americans. They had a hard time trying to live in an Anglo-American culture because of the prejudiced attitudes they faced. For example, many Anglos thought that Mexicans were only good when they worked in the fields.

C13. Unfair attitudes toward the Mexican-Americans made it hard for them to get better-paying jobs in the cities. Those who lived in cities often lived in poorer neighborhoods called *barrios*. Living in these areas was good because the Mexican-Americans felt comfortable living with their own people. What are the advantages and disadvantages of living in any isolated area?

C14. Many Mexican-Americans did not move to the cities. Instead they remained on the fields. But work became scarce in Mexico, so Mexicans began crossing the border in order to work in the fields. Because they would work for lower wages, they got most of the available jobs. Aliens are people who come from another country. These *illegal aliens* were called *wetbacks.*

C15. Now farm workers are fighting for better working and living conditions. They have organized a *union* in order to fight for their rights. This union was formed to organize the workers into a strong group. One man, Cesar Chavez, has been a strong leader of these people and their union. He has helped them stand up for their rights. Now the Mexican-Americans can begin to be treated equally yet still take pride in their culture.

UNIT D—ASIANS

D1. California has the largest Chinese population of all the states in America. The Chinese people began entering around 1850 when the news of the *Gold Rush* spread throughout the world. At this time, the Chinese people were having a hard time supporting their families at home. Many Chinese men came to California and set up *gold claims* (digging sites) in hopes of becoming rich.

D2. In the beginning of the Gold Rush, there was lots of gold in the California hills. But there was also much greed and competition to get that gold. Foreigners were seen as having no rights to American land or its riches. The Chinese were finally forced off their gold claims. The only other work that they could do was to work on the transcontinental railroad. This was back-breaking, dangerous work.

D3. The Chinese proved to be good workers on the railroad. But soon it was completed, leaving them without jobs and without money to go home to China. As agriculture developed, many Chinese took to the fields. Some became domestic workers. Eventually others set up their own businesses. For example, they opened restaurants, laundries, and other small shops.

D4.   Chinatowns were made up mostly of single Chinese men. They did not intend to stay in the United States. They were here to work so they could send money home to their families. These men lived together because it was more comfortable for them. It was more like home. Also, increasing prejudice and misunderstanding encouraged the Chinese to live in these towns.

D5.   In 1943 the Chinese were allowed to become citizens. Since then they have suffered much less prejudice than they had in the past. The Chinese people have contributed to making America a culturally rich nation. Chinatowns, especially in Los Angeles and San Francisco, have become some of the largest cultural centers in California. In what ways can you see the cultural influence of the Chinese people?

D6   This land was attractive not only to the Chinese people. Another Asian group also had reasons for wanting to come here. These people were the Japanese. Some fled Japan in order to avoid being drafted into the Japanese army. When they arrived, many found work in the fields.

D7.   At this time, much of the California land was being used to grow food. Sugar beet crops required a lot of people working in the fields in order to produce them. This attracted Japanese workers to the area. In fact, many were able to save enough money to buy land of their own.

D8.   The Japanese knew many important farming skills before they came to America. Using these methods here, they were very successful at turning useless land into rich, fertile soil. Their success worried many Anglo-Americans. Can you think of any reasons why this success caused so much worry? Discuss.

D9.   While many Japanese families worked hard on the land, others tried to get better jobs in the cities. Like other minorities, they too had to deal with much discrimination. While some were more comfortable living with their own people, others were attracted to living in more *Americanized* communities. What does "Americanized" mean? Half the group try to come up with the possible advantages of Americanization, and the other half of the group think of possible disadvantages. Then discuss.

D10. In 1941, the United States and Japan were at war. The United States feared that the Japanese living in America would not be loyal to their new country. Even though many fought in the U.S. Army, the government still was uncertain. The Japanese-Americans who lived in the west coast states were placed in camps. Many lost their jobs, their homes, and their *dignity*. In what ways did they lose their dignity?

UNIT E—BLACKS

E1.   Black people were the first minority who were forced to come to America. Originally they came of their *own free will,* but by the late 1600s slavery became a profitable business. Blacks were brought from Africa to the east coast on large British ships. Many died along the way from disease, hunger, and cruel treatment. In fact, some even threw themselves overboard, preferring to die.

E2.   Slaves were sold as property. Many large-plantation owners wanted slaves because they were cheap labor. A slave owner could do anything he wanted with his slaves. Although the slaves were helpless, they did everything they could to make their lives livable. They would act as the Americans wanted them to in order to avoid punishment. At this time, there were no laws to give the black people equal rights. The Americans thought the blacks preferred to be slaves so they could be taken care of.

E3.   The slaves did not outwardly fight against this system of slavery. Instead they tried to get around it by acting in a certain way. Many times they pretended to be devoted servants or happy-go-lucky clowns. By doing this, they avoided trouble. In this way the white masters felt in control of them. Those who tried to fight against slavery were always severely punished and often killed. What would you do if you were a slave?

E4.   In 1780 the northern states ended slavery. But slavery remained in the South. Now the slaves had some hope of freedom. Many tried to escape to the North. The underground railroad became an important passageway to a new free way of life. Both whites and free blacks helped the slaves escape the South. Those who worked to abolish (end) slavery were called *abolitionists*. They gave speeches and wrote many books to help their cause. But words alone were not enough.

E5.   War broke out between the northern states and the southern states. This war was called the *Civil War*. The southern states wanted to form their own government and make their own rules. The northern states wanted to keep all the states together under one government. After much fighting, the North won. What do you think our country would be like if the South had won? Discuss.

E6.   Blacks continued to move northward. But they faced discrimination wherever they went. They were still looked upon as an *inferior* race. They were treated like second-class citizens. Although laws had been passed long ago that gave equal rights to all men, this was not so. Blacks were continually separated from the white men. They were kept from sharing everything from jobs to drinking fountains.

E7.   Even when the blacks and whites were fighting together as Americans during World War II, they were kept apart. For example, army training camps were separated into two units, one for blacks and one for whites. Another example of segregation was that black children had to go to separate schools. These schools were usually not as good as schools for white children.

E8.   About 1960 a new movement began in order to help the black people gain equal rights. This was called the *civil rights movement*. Black people were tired of being kept apart from American society. They wanted to have equal treatment in all aspects of American life. The most important leader at this time was *Dr. Martin Luther King, Jr.* He gave a famous speech, "I Have a Dream." What do you think he meant?

E9.   The Civil Rights Act was passed because it was believed that all people should have their rights protected. It is not good for a nation to have its people fighting among themselves. This is not democracy. And democracy is what our nation was first built on—equal treatment for all. Guaranteeing equal treatment and equal rights was the building block of America, but not until 1965 did it become *law of the land.*

E10. The government passed the Civil Rights Act in 1965. Its purpose was to end *racial discrimination*. It tried to do this in four ways. The first way stated that all people had the right to use public facilities. The second way was to legally make businesses end any discrimination practices. The third way gave all people equal voting rights. And finally, the fourth way ended any discrimination having to do with jobs. But changing people's attitudes was harder than changing laws. Why would this be so?

E11. Discrimination was still practiced in the United States even though the Civil Rights Act had become a national law. This created much bitterness from many frustrated minorities. For example, a bloody riot (1965) broke out in Watts, a black section of Los Angeles. It lasted six days. Thirty-five people were killed and most of these were blacks. Movements were organized to unite blacks in the struggle for equal rights. Some believed that the only way to solve the problem was through violence; others did not.

E12. The struggle for equal rights has been a slow, frustrating process. Many Americans are only beginning to respect the laws of equal rights. If you were to travel through any part of the country, you would probably still see a lot of unfair treatment. For example, many people still face job discrimination and unequal *employment opportunities*. Many minority students need to drop out of school in order to find work, and, for many, school is a hopeless place to be.

E13. Much had been done since 1960 to give the blacks equal rights. Many laws have been passed to try to bring all minorities together as Americans. One of these laws had to do with busing kids to different schools. Black children would go with white children to white schools, and white children would go with black children to black schools. In this way, children of different races could learn to work together and have an equal educational opportunity. How do you feel about the busing issue? Discuss the advantages and disadvantages of busing.

E14. Busing kids to different schools brought on many problems. Besides having to go long distances to school, many of the black kids had not had the advantages in school that the white kids had. This made it hard for them to keep up in class. Also, each group felt more comfortable with their old friends so they would stay together. One solution to help lessen this problem was the jigsaw. The jigsaw is this learning method that you have been using the last few weeks. It was made to help kids of all backgrounds work together. How have you helped this method work in your classroom?

E15. With the ending of slavery, thousands of blacks came to the West seeking a better way of life. About one-quarter of the nation's black people live in the West. Although groups such as the Ku Klux Klan still exist to keep white superiority, blacks have overcome much of this *racism.* Through the struggle for equal rights, they are now beginning to have the same opportunities in jobs and in schools. In fact, discrimination against any race is against the law. Do you think discrimination has been totally eliminated? Discuss the concept of *reverse discrimination.*

UNIT F—CONCLUSION

F1. Stevie Wonder is a famous black musician of today. The words in his songs have a special meaning to all of us. His song "Black Man" is a good example of how all groups of people have helped contribute to the growth of America. "We pledge allegiance, all of our lives, to the magic colors, red, blue, and white. But we all must be given the liberty that we defend, for with justice not for all men, history will repeat again. It's time we learned this world was made for all men."

F2. We have seen that our nation is made up of many different groups. Each has played an important part in America's history. For example, an Indian woman (Sacajawea) showed early explorers their way through the wilderness. Later when the new settlers arrived, Indians showed them how to survive on the land. Also, Indian leaders have helped improve the lives of many Indians. Today, one important leader of this movement is Dennis Banks.

F3. The Mexican culture has become an important part of the culture of the western states. The language, clothing, food, and dances are just a few of their contributions. These Mexicans have also worked hard in the fields, producing much of the food we eat. One of the most important leaders today who helped these farm workers gain equal rights is Cesar Chavez.

F4. The white people, too, have given us many things to be proud of. Among some of them are Ben Franklin's discovery of electricity and Alexander Graham Bell's invention of the telephone. Also, Susan B. Anthony was one of the key figures of the women's suffrage movement. It is because of people like her that women have the right to vote.

The Asians were the people who linked the east and west coasts. They worked on the transcontinental railroad. They also shared their skills in the martial arts and have contributed much to the field of medicine and cooking, to mention just a few.

F5. Like the Asians, black people have contributed to the field of medicine. For example, Dr. Dennis Williams was the first to successfully perform open-heart surgery. Dr. Charles Drew was the founder of the Red Cross blood bank. Another man, Matthew Hansen, was the first person to set foot on the North Pole. And when the slaves were fleeing to freedom, it was Harriet Tubman who helped them escape on the underground railroad. And, remember the important leader in the blacks' civil rights movement, Dr. Martin Luther King, Jr.

F6. If you look around the classroom, you will find that no two people are alike. Some have different-colored skin, some are tall, some are short, everyone is a special individual. Make a circle and have everyone in your group put their right hand in the center. Notice how your hand is different from all the others. Talk about the differences. Do these differences tell you something about what kind of person each of you are? Repeat this exercise with your jigsaw group.

F7. Sometimes we generalize our feelings about one person to all people with some of the same characteristics. *Stereotypes* are dangerous because they close our minds to what individuals are really like. Let's take a look at what happens to Frank's stereotyped ideas. When he was young, he once tasted some beets and he thought they were horrible. When he saw tomatoes, their color reminded him of those horrible beets. He wouldn't touch them. As time passed, he began to hate everything that was red, even strawberry ice cream. In fact, he wouldn't even talk to any people with red hair. How has Frank's stereotype closed his mind to what really is? Discuss.

F8. *Prejudice* is a feeling or belief that a person has about something. For example, a boy named Frank hated red-haired people. He didn't have any reason or thought behind his dislike for them. He just couldn't stand to be around anybody with red hair. They were horrible, just like the red beets that had tasted so awful. Often people are prejudiced against other people, especially minorities and ethnic groups who seem different to them. In order to end prejudice, all Americans must learn that their differences are what make this country strong.

F9. Can you think of how we become prejudiced? Are we born with it or is it learned? The fact is that prejudice is learned. Most of the time prejudice is not taught to us directly. It is built into our school books, our newspapers, our television programs, and even given to us by the people whom we are closest to. Often the same fact can be said in different ways, depending on a person's point of view. For example, you might see two different movies about the battle of Little Big Horn. Each one may show a slanted view of the fact. One may show Custer's final attempt to wipe out the "savage" Indians. The other may show the Indians finally taking revenge on the "cruelty" of the white man.

F10. A lot of times people don't realize that they are prejudiced against others. They are not aware that there could be another side to the story. One way to overcome this problem is to become aware that people in our country are free. This means that they have the right to hold on to their cultural values and to have equal treatment in whatever they do. This is a pluralistic country. As we look into the future, we can see that everyone in our country will be needed to pull together. We will need all of our strength to solve such universal problems as hunger, poverty, pollution, energy and water shortages, and over-population. We are all in it together, and you are needed as much as anyone else to make this world a better place for all humankind.

APPENDIX C
GROUP-PROCESS SHEET

Note to the teacher: This sheet is designed as a handout for the students to help them become familiar with some important aspects of group process. You may also want to use some of the ideas from this sheet in a "Group-Process Bulletin Board."

Some important things to remember about group-process:

It is important to let the person who is talking know that you are listening to what he or she is saying. Some ways you can do this are:

> nodding
> smiling
> asking questions.

There are some other ways you can show you are listening. Can you think of any?

When you are using the jigsaw method, you do many different things each day, and you need to have time for each of them. Try and keep an idea of how much time is left so you don't run out before you are done with everything.

At the end of each day you will have a process discussion. You will answer several questions about what happened in your group that day and discuss them. These discussions are important because how well you will be able to learn the material depends on how well your group works together. Try to help see what problems your group is having, and come up with suggestions for solving them in these discussions.

This is a list that you can use to have students process what happens in their group each day. Have them discuss the first three questions most days. The other questions provide additional focus on specific issues. You may want to do one a day, or whatever you have time for.

(1) What one word would you use to describe how the group was today?

_____

(2) What one word would describe the way you would like the group to be? _____

(3) Is everyone participating?
     Yes, always _____ Usually _____ Occasionally _____ Rarely _____
     No, never _____ If not, why not?

_____

(4) Are you (everyone in group) trying to make each other feel good?
     If not, what are you doing?
     Yes, always _____ Usually _____ Occasionally _____ Rarely _____
     No, never _____

(5) Are you trying to help each other feel able to talk and say what you
     think?
     Yes, always _____ Usually _____ Occasionally _____ Rarely _____
     No, never _____

(6) Are you listening to each other?
     Yes, always _____ Usually _____ Occasionally _____ Rarely _____
     No, never _____

(7) Are you showing you are listening by nodding at each other?
     Yes, always _____ Usually _____ Occasionally _____ Rarely _____
     No, never _____

(8) Are you saying "That's good" to each other when you like some-
     thing?
     Yes, always _____ Usually _____ Occasionally _____ Rarely _____
     No, never _____

(9) Are you asking each other questions?
     Yes, always _____ Usually _____ Occasionally _____ Rarely _____
     No, never _____

(10) Are you listening and really trying to answer these questions?
     Yes, always _____ Usually _____ Occasionally _____ Rarely _____

(11) Are you paying attention to each other?
     Yes, always _____ Usually _____ Occasionally _____ Rarely _____

(12) Is any one person talking most of the time? Yes _____ No _____

(13) Is there a way to have a group where everyone talks about equally?
     Yes _____ No _____

APPENDIX D
TEACHER TRAINING WORKSHOPS

Teachers who want to use the jigsaw technique in their classrooms can profit from specialized training to hasten their own and their students adaptation to the approach. While there is nothing magical about the procedures—indeed, they are quite simple—it is highly recommended that teachers interested in mastering this technique do more than read about it. Since many of the learnings are experiential as well as cognitive, it would be beneficial for teachers to experience what it is like to work in small groups in order to supplement their understanding of the theory and research that underlies the jigsaw.

It is clear that educators are well aware of the benefits of in-service workshops to supplement reading about innovative teaching techniques. Thus in the two years since our work has been publicized, we have received scores of requests from counselors, teachers, and curriculum co-ordinators to perform the kind of workshops we used for training the teachers who participated in our research project. While we were able to accommodate many school systems, the task soon became too difficult. Thus here we will describe in some detail the kind of teacher training workshops we have been conducting, in the hope that school systems will be able to train their own teachers with little or no outside consultation. Even those who have no intention of conducting or attending such a workshop should study this section because we believe that it might enrich the reader's understanding of some of the underlying assumptions of the jigsaw technique.

Ideally, we would recommend about five days of training for a teacher to reach the point where he or she could employ the jigsaw method of teaching with a great deal of skill and confidence. Unfortunately, most in-service workshops are one-day affairs, and so our objectives must be limited. Nonetheless, a great deal can be learned in one day.

If you were asked to lead a one-day introductory workshop on the jigsaw method, what objectives would you reasonably expect to attain? Minimally, you would try to provide the experiences that would enable the teachers to gain a greater cognitive understanding of the benefit of the occasional use of cooperative strategies, an idea of how these strategies may be implemented, and a beginning notion of how to deal with many of the problems that may arise during the implementation phase. In addition, you would want to provide the teachers with an opportunity to experience for themselves teambuilding activities and group processing exercises, in order to develop their group dynamics skills. This would also help the teachers understand and empathize with their students and what they might be experiencing in their own small groups. In addition, team-building activities during the workshops would allow the teachers the opportunity to get to know each other better and to discover new resources among their colleagues; providing a structure for teachers to share ideas and give each other support occurs far too seldom at most in-service workshops. In our experience it is appreciated and welcomed by the teachers. Moreover, forming support systems can be of great significance for the jigsaw teachers.

To accomplish all of these objectives in a one-day workshop requires a full schedule of carefully planned, well-designed activities. Following is one of the workshop designs which we have found successful.

The workshop description is presented in two columns. In the left column are detailed directions that have been important to us in conducting an effective workshop. In the right column is the rationale for doing what is described in the directions. The reader who has conducted many in-service workshops and has developed a style that suits her individually, as well as her own rationale, may wish to adapt some of the instructions to her own style and may even wish to skim this chapter. Less experienced leaders will want to read much more carefully.

INSTRUCTIONS	RATIONALE
8:30–8:45 **15 minutes**	
1a. Coffee and time for casual talk. The leader, or facilitator, should announce that the workshop will begin at 8:45, since there are a few teachers who have not yet arrived.	1b. It is usually necessary to start the first session a few minutes late to await late arrivals. To announce when the workshop will actually begin alleviates any anxiety and annoyance caused by uncertainty about time.
8:45–9:00 **15 minutes**	
2a. Brief lecture about the need for developing cooperation in the classroom, and a description of the day's schedule. The subjects discussed in the mini-lecture may be drawn from the beginning of chapter one. Topics might include: (a) the unwanted consequences of a competitive society; (b) the squandering of human resources	2b. A rough idea of the schedule helps the participants feel more comfortable by letting them know what they may expect. We also give the mini-lecture, even though participants are rarely settled enough to attend to it carefully. The mini-lecture is given informally without a prepared text in order to create a relaxed atmosphere. To see the

(students) in a teacher-dominated classroom; (c) problems minority students have in newly integrated schools and a possible relation to competitive classroom environment; and (d) how cooperation strategies might help.

"authorities" delivering information in the traditional classroom manner allows the participants to ease into the topic of the day, and gives them a cognitive framework within which to understand why they are being encouraged to participate in the next activities.

9:00—9:20
20 minutes

3a. Directions: "As you all know, before any group activity in the classroom can work, the teacher needs to prepare the class in such a way that they are ready to work together. In a little while, we are going to be discussing techniques that you've found effective in your teaching, but first we need to engage in some teambuilding activities so that when we get into discussion groups these groups will be able to work more effectively. We want you to experience these activities, to see if you might use them in your classroom.

"First, we need quickly to get better acquainted with the resources we have here. The first activity will help us begin to know each other."

If the number of participants is less than fifteen, have each person, beginning with the workshop leader, give his name, a brief description of his professional background and interest, and a summary of what he hopes to learn during the day.

With a larger group of teachers (15 to 20) give each person a piece of newsprint with a felt marker and ask him to draw a picture or write something that will represent him in two dimensions—first, his professional life and, second, his personal interests. For example, if somebody plays a lot of tennis during leisure hours, he might draw himself play-

3b. We have found that the sooner the participants begin to get to know each other, to get comfortable, and to feel accepted in the larger group, the sooner their energies can be directed toward the content at hand. Most people feel some discomfort and anxiety at the beginning of a workshop. If this is not attended to early, some participants may become restless and resistant to the activities. In attempting to help the participants move rapidly past this initial feeling of isolation, anxiety, and resistance, it may be necessary to make them temporarily even more uncomfortable by encouraging them to get to know the very people they might have felt awkward talking to when they first entered the room. The structure suggested here will be experienced as embarrassing for a moment, as would any activity designed to "break the ice." Once the ice has been broken, however, a relaxed, cooperative atmosphere can readily be established.

The leader can decrease any resistance to a structured ice-breaking activity by discussing the parallels to their teaching situations back in their classrooms. Teachers are often faced with a situation in which it is hard to induce a positive outlook in students toward some activity they know the students will enjoy and learn from in the long run.

ing tennis or he might divide a pie into the amount of time he spends in different roles, e.g., parent, teacher, athlete, chauffeur, etc. Ask participants to do this quickly, nonverbally, taking only five minutes to complete their "advertisements" of who they are. Then ask them to put their names somewhere prominently on the newsprint and, without any talking, walk around holding the newsprint in front of them, reading other people's while others read theirs.

They should mill around the circle, and should try to remember some people who share common interests and with whom they may want to make contact later. If you think they will be too uncomfortable with silence, they may be permitted to ask each other a few questions.

It is important that participants avoid choosing their best friends, thus opting for comfort at the expense of increasing their range of contacts and experiences.

The teachers are then asked to find one person they don't know well, sit down together, and introduce themselves.

9:20–9:40
20 minutes

4a. After a couple of minutes, interrupt and give the following directions:

"In order to establish a cooperative classroom atmosphere at the beginning of the year, it is very important that the students get to know each other. One useful technique is to have them pair up to interview each other in a special way. We are going to do that exercise in just a moment. Not only will it give us an inside view of what we can do with our own students, it also will be helpful in facilitating our own acquaintance process right here in this room. What I would like each of you to do is to think of three questions that would help you get to know your partner better. The temptation may be

4b. Most of the rationale here is contained within the directions. The more the leader can share the rationale behind what he is doing, the more willing and able the participants are to follow the directions. We are all more likely to be interested in an exercise if we understand its practical application in our lives. Teachers know their students need to develop the quality of their listening skills. This exercise helps them experience what it is like to work directly on that skill.

The directions for this exercise are undoubtedly long. However, it is probably better to give the directions all at once, rather than to try to interrupt the group, wait for simply to ask your partner questions like 'Where do you live?' and 'Do you know so and so?' Then both of you might continue discussing in a more or less superficial way that person whom you happen to know in common. While these questions might help people get acquainted, it takes a long time to develop much of a feeling of empathy for the other person. Many of us have spent time with a variety of people on different occasions and still have little understanding of them or how they experience the world. What I would like for us to do is think of three questions that will really help us get to know our partners better. Effective questions might be like these: Think of a close friend of yours; if you were to ask that close friend what she likes best about you, what might she say? If I were to ask that person what she wishes you would change about yourself, what might she say? When were you happiest in the last month? What has irritated you most in the last week? You might want to use some of the questions I have just suggested, or you might want to think up some of your own. Please take a minute silently to think of any three questions which will help you to get to know your partner better.''

After a moment's pause, continue: "We will also make this interviewing process into a listening exercise. In order to learn effective communication, your students will have to practice effective listening. Effective or 'active' listening by the listener not only helps the speaker to know that she is communicating effectively, but also helps her to feel that the listener cares enough to attend to her closely and that they are in contact with each other. To encourage this

them to be silent, and give them more directions. With a large group it is difficult to get everyone to stop talking at the same time.

By providing them with a specific number of questions to ask, the leader has defined the task in such a way there is less likelihood that a participant will wander off the subject. With students, asking them to write down their questions greatly increases the likelihood that the questions will be carefully composed.

active listening, it is advisable for the listener occasionally to rephrase or clarify what the person speaking has just said. In order to practice that in our interviews here, the listener should keep trying to summarize the essence of the speaker's comments until the speaker says, 'Yes, you understand what I have said.' Then we may proceed to the next question. So, after the question has been answered, rephrase it, trying to get to the meaning of what the person has said by expanding it a little. When the interviewee indicates that, yes, you have understood her, go on to ask a new question. 'The speaker will, of course, only reveal as much as she feels comfortable in revealing. If the interviewer is tolerant, accepting, and interested, the speaker will probably enjoy sharing herself. However, we are not offering any prizes to those who respond most intimately.'

"You will need to listen closely to your partner and to remember what she says because, in effect, you will be tested on it. That is, in a few minutes you will be introducing her to another two couples by sharing what you have learned about her. In the classroom, this extra twist increases student motivation to listen carefully.

"You will have five minutes for one of you to interview your partner. Then I will announce that you should switch so that the interviewee can become the interviewer. Begin asking your three questions."

When participants are asked to do something they may experience as threatening, or to reveal themselves before they feel safe (e.g., in the interviewing situation), it is important to give the directions in such a way that they can choose with a sense of dignity to participate only superficially, or even not at all. There should be no pressure or coercion by the leader of the group to do any activity which would emotionally upset the participant (teacher or student). It is the leader's responsibility to make sure that the participants have a dignified "out."

This is not to say that the leader should discourage participants from choosing to do something that would make them uncomfortable at the beginning (e.g., meeting other teachers, or sharing their ideas). On the contrary. If they choose to tolerate that discomfort in order to learn something, fine. However, it is equally fine if they choose not to do something that would make them uncomfortable. What is important is that the atmosphere be one in which either choice is actively supported.

When a leader is moving large groups of people from one activity to another, it is very important to give them a one- or two-minute warning. This warning must be announced loudly while participants are still talking. The information about the time remaining will give them a chance to end their discussion.

9:40—9:55
15 minutes

5a. Directions: "We are going to take a break in fifteen minutes. First, in just a moment, would each couple join two other couples near them, preferably joining with people you don't know very well. Then would you introduce your partner and what you learned about her, trying to be sensitive to how much she would want you to reveal."

After seven or eight minutes, when the groups seem to be about finished with their introductions, give the following summary of how this can be transferred to the classroom. "We had you join the six-person group, with a partner as a support base. In the classroom, before having discussion groups begin talking about some topic, it is very useful to have the students first write down two ideas about the topic, and then share those ideas with one other person. Writing down the ideas gives them something specific to say, and rehearsing the expression of those ideas with a partner makes it easier for them to participate in the groups. This morning, as is possible in the classroom, we used the interviewing in pairs as a 'warm-up,' since it is easier first to make contact with just one person, and then, with that person, to join four strangers.

"In the last few minutes before the break, would you discuss what you gave up in order to be here today, and what you hope to gain from the workshop. For example, I have piles of term papers on my desk that need to be read and graded. I gave up getting that done to come here. I came because I am excited about sharing my ideas about facilitating a cooperative classroom atmosphere, and learning from you what has been work-

5b. The session has been going for almost an hour, and the participants will be wanting a break. For design purposes, the break fits better in a few minutes, so to avoid distraction it is important to let them know they can anticipate a break soon.

Again, we give them permission to be a little cautious about how much they disclose. Ideally, the depth of disclosure should be enough for them to feel empathy for each other but not enough for anyone to become embarrassed.

The leader should interrupt gently but firmly. There may be one or two groups that haven't quite finished, just as there may be one or two groups who finished early and are beginning to get bored. The leader must sense the proper time to intervene even at the expense of cutting off a discussion before it is finished. She should offer reassurances; e.g., "If you are not quite finished, you may want to continue during the break."

Five or ten minutes of discussion on these final two topics can save a lot of time later. At the beginning of an in-service workshop, much teacher energy may be devoted to wishing they were doing something else that is very pressing. This creates resistance to focusing on what is happening. The mere sharing of their ambivalence helps teachers move past their resistance, to then enter into a positive discussion of what their goals for the workshop are. The clearer they are about their objectives, the more likely it is these objectives will be met.

ing in your classrooms. Take a few minutes before the break to share what you gave up in order to come today and what you hope to gain from the workshop. I will tell you when the break begins. Go ahead and start."

9:55—10:20
15—25 minutes

6a. Ask them to remember what group they are in, and then announce a break of from ten to twenty minutes, depending upon how tight your schedule is.

6b. Although times are stated with precision in the left-hand column, some flexibility is usually warranted. Consequently, we are usually at least ten minutes behind schedule by now, so the break is not as long as it would seem!

While the group is taking a break, let's reflect on what has been accomplished this past hour. The participants have had a short talk on the need for cooperation in the classroom and also were told the day's schedule. They have gotten briefly acquainted with the resources in the room, have made a little contact with everyone, and will be able to approach people during the break that they think they might want to know better. They have had the opportunity to develop a support base with one other person, a partner with whom they could more effectively enter the six-person group. They have had a chance to express their possible ambivalence about attending the workshop and have had a chance to focus on what they hope to get out of it. The leader has also shown how the exercises might be used in the classroom, and has sensitized the participants to several issues related to leading teambuilding activities. Now let's return to the workshop.

10:20—11:30
70 minutes

7a. About three minutes before the end of the break, announce that we will be beginning in a few minutes. Ask them to return to their six-person groups and chat for a few minutes. Then use the following introduction:

"As you may know, it is very important, when you have students working in groups in a classroom, for them to understand something

7b. While we haven't used it here, we like to begin this session to show the movie, "What's New in the Schools" (Carousel Films*) a CBS documentary showing two opposite poles of educational teaching styles: on the one end a very control-oriented, "traditional" teacher,

———————

*This film may be rented from Carousel Films, New York.

about their group dynamics. It is necessary for the students to possess the skills to change their group process in such a way as to make it more productive and rewarding. To develop these skills, a very useful activity is one called *fish-bowling*. For this activity, one group sits on the inside and talks about some topic while another group sits on the outside, watches very carefully the group dynamics occurring on the inside, and later gets on the inside and reacts to the first group's process.

"We are going to do that here to give you a chance to see what that experience is like. The first group is going to be in the center and will be discussing the topics 'What type of students seem to gain from competitive environments' and 'When competitive strategies in the classroom help increase learning.' While the first group is discussing that topic, the second group over here will be sitting around the outside of the first group, observing that group on several criteria. I will explain those criteria in a moment. First, would each group combine with one other group. Now, would one six-person group sit in the middle and would those in the paired group move your chairs to surround that group?" (Pause while they form into inner and outer groups.)

"Now all the groups on the inside are going to discuss situations in which competition in the classroom may help increase learning and, in particular, what type of students seem to benefit most from competitive environments. The group on the outside will be watching the group on the inside on the basis of the criteria listed on the newsprint.

"The first of these is: (1) What is the 'climate of listening'? Are people nodding at each other? Is there eye contact? Are they re-

and on the other end an open classroom with a very humanistic approach. We show the film in order to stimulate a discussion of the problems with both traditional education and freer learning environments. Our hope is that we can find a position somewhere in the middle with educational strategies which might be more effective for the students. Since many readers will not have this film available, we will not discuss in detail how it is used except to say that we would draw on topics from the film for fish-bowl discussions.

Again, most of the rationale for this exercise is given within the directions. The participants are learning on three levels. First, they are learning by experiencing (as participants) the process of the various exercises. They will now empathize better when their students participate in similar activities. Second, as participants they are learning from each other the *content* of the topics. Third, they are learning as they watch the leader model effective behavior, and as they listen to him explain why he is doing what he is doing (e.g., what pitfalls he is avoiding, and what kind of an atmosphere he is promoting).

The particular topic chosen for discussion is not crucial. It must merely be of interest, and one that would relate to effective teaching. In this case we chose topics which would indicate that we are aware that competition is often a useful motivator and that it may have detrimental effects. Too often we waste a lot of energy arguing issues rather than exploring where each view might have some merit.

phrasing what other people have been saying?

"(2) Who seems to be taking leadership? Does she seem to be helping the group have an effective discussion? For example, who initiates in order to help the group get moving? Who is helping the group move along when it has reached consensus? Who is helping the group by summarizing what people have been saying so that it can proceed? Who is helping them stick to the topic?

"(3) Is everyone able to participate? Watch for whether all of the members are invited to share their ideas or whether they need to interrupt in order to speak. Not everyone may want to share, and that is O.K., as long as they know they are welcome to.

"(4) What's the energy level? Are people sitting up, leaning forward, appearing to be interested and eager to share, or at times do people sit way back and withdraw? And what do you think is causing that?

"In addition to those four dimensions you can attend to any other aspects of group dynamics you would like to, such as who seems to be talking to whom in the group. Make notes on what processes you observe because in ten minutes you will be getting into the center and discussing their group process.

"Will the group in the center now begin talking about situations in which competition seems to help learning and for which type of students is this particularly so? You have ten minutes."

After ten minutes give a one-minute warning, then say: "Stop your discussion now. Will the first group, which was inside, move to the outside and will the second group move to the inside? Then the group that was observing will begin discussing the process of the first group. Try to be as constructive as you can by focusing on specific behaviors and what you think the effects of those behaviors were. Rather than talking about somebody's 'stupid comment' or 'authoritarian voice,' talk about the behaviors in nonevaluative and nonjudgmental terms.

"Remember, it is not easy to be at your best while you are being observed. While it is important to share your observations, it is equally important to do so in a caring, constructive manner, just as you would want your students to do.

"The first group will now begin to observe the process of the second group. Again, watch for these four questions: What is the climate of listening? Who is leading and how effective are they? Is everybody invited to participate? What is the energy level of the group?"

After five minutes give a one-minute warning, then say: "Switch places now and begin. You'll have five minutes."

Then, after a one-minute warning, "Your five minutes are up. Groups that were sitting on the outside listening to your group being discussed, notice your emotional reactions right now. It is likely that some of you are feeling somewhat defensive even if they were saying mostly positive things about your group. Your group may be temporarily more cohesive because it is having to face outside critique. If you do this in your classroom you may not even want to let the critiquing go more than two minutes at the beginning. In two minutes most of the comments will be quite positive. Moreover, the early positive effects, or early learnings, of fish-bowling are not from the critiques as much as from the attempts of the group on the inside to be an effective team because it is in the center being observed by another group.

"All of you have probably already noticed how much better you were attending to your group behavior when that other group was observing you. While it may have seemed forced to try to be 'good' group members, after a few days students are able to be spontaneous, to be themselves, while still trying to make their group an effective one. Later, when the students have a higher level of trust and when they have the skills to communicate the feedback in a way that is constructive, the teacher might let the critiquing extend to five or ten minutes.

"Will the second group stay inside the circle and now discuss which type of students seems to be hurt by a competitive atmosphere and in what situations a cooperative mode might increase the learning in a class? You will have ten minutes to discuss this while the group on the outside continues taking notes on your group's process."

After ten minutes give a one-minute warning, then say: "Will you stop, please? Will the group in the center now move to the outside and the group on the outside now move to the center and discuss for five minutes the second group's process?"

At the end of this, summarize the learnings, remarking on what you noticed about group dynamics and what made a group go well and what hindered it.

Then briefly ask people how they experienced that exercise, and try to relate their comments to actual ways that such an exercise might be used in the classroom.

11:30—11:45 Question-and-answer period.

11:45—1:30   Lunch.

1:30—1:40
10 minutes

8a. Ask the teachers to return to their six-person groups and to discuss for ten minutes any issues raised by the lectures or by the morning's activities.

8b. This time is primarily for the participants to share any thoughts and opinions they might have had over lunch. It also provides an opportunity for them to get settled into their groups and ready to work on the next task.

1:40—1:50
10 minutes

9a. The next step is to provide the teachers with a jigsaw experience. Hand the packet of workshop materials to one person in each group, who will be designated the leader for the next exercise. Then ask the leader to hand each person in her group one of the paragraphs. Explain: "Each person will have a paragraph covering some issue associated with the use of the jigsaw technique. Study your paragraph for five minutes and think about how you can best teach the group about that issue.

"For example, the people with the second paragraph will teach about 'the importance of team-building.' To prepare for leading a discussion on that topic, they will read through the paragraph, see what the ideas are, and then relate them to their own classroom experiences. During the five-minute planning time, they will jot down some of the ways they can elicit group discussion on those ideas. For instance, they may note they want to begin their section with a fantasy of the beginning of the school year. This fantasy might include how the kids are going to be feeling about each other and how getting to know each other

9b. This exercise is the most important of the workshop. In it the teachers first see the jigsaw process at work. They will learn about the jigsaw process both by experiencing it and by discussing it. Because the teachers are actively involved, they are able to absorb the necessary information more easily and efficiently.

Since all, in turn, will be responsible for teaching some topic, as group members they will tend to be supportive of the topic leaders, and will try to make discussion productive.

will be important. Or they may want to begin with a brief role-playing of a disruptive, ineffective group. Or they may merely want to begin with asking questions about why teambuilding exercises might be useful at the beginning of the year. The goal is to draw the members into a discussion during which they teach each other about the importance of teambuilding."

Conclude the directions by telling the teachers again that at the end of a five-minute preparation period, each will take a turn leading a five-minute discussion on his or her particular topic.

1:50—2:25
35 minutes

10a. The group leader should designate a timekeeper since the group as a whole will only have thirty minutes to cover all six topics. Remind participants that each will have only five minutes. Then the person with the first paragraph should begin.

While the groups are working, you move around answering questions and observing the dynamics of each group. You should make comments about group process to the leader of the group, quietly suggesting, for example, that the group should now move on to the next topic. If you notice, at the beginning, that members are still preparing their topic rather than listening to the discussion, you may point that out. If the participants are talking to the topic leader, encourage them to talk to the group as a whole.

10b. The group timekeeper will help the group focus on its task and keep the discussion progressing. Here is the opportunity for the facilitator to point out the importance of time limits in increasing group productivity.

This exercise is designed to help teachers help each other do the best job of teaching they can, and also to increase interest in the topic. It should become apparent to them that they already know much of the information necessary for them to use the jigsaw method. They should also discover that as a group they have many resources for helping each other learn to be effective facilitators in their classrooms.

Initially, groups need assistance in becoming productive. This assistance should come primarily from within the group; hence the facilitator works through the leaders to validate their authority, instead of giving direct assistance.

2:25—2:45
20 minutes

11a. As each group finishes, announce that there will be a break after each person writes down five things he noticed about the group process. Encourage participants to refer to the process questions on the newsprint which were used for the fishbowl exercise in the morning. Tell them to spend about five minutes working quietly, and then to take a fifteen-minute break.

11b. Since there will be a break, it is not essential that all the groups finish at the same time. However, the facilitator should not let participants work more than five minutes into their break, because they will need at least a ten-minute break in order to keep working effectively.

The reasons for having participants write their observations about group process are twofold. First, it will help them to remember their ideas for a discussion after the break. Second, it increases the likelihood that these thoughts will be verbalized in discussion.

2:45—2:55
10 minutes

12a. Have participants return to their groups and give directions along the following lines: "In a moment you will have five minutes to discuss how your group worked together in the jigsaw exercise. I'd like you to do this by telling the others what you liked about what they did, and what you thought they could do better. If you wish, refer to your notes, but try not to merely read them to the others. This will help keep the discussion flowing spontaneously.

"So you can also learn how the other groups functioned, we are going to fish-bowl this discussion. This will encourage the group on the inside to critique itself thoroughly and also to attend to its present group process. The group on the outside will again take notes on the process of the other group, using the four questions posted on the board this morning. Members of the outside group will then move to the center and will have five minutes to give their observations."

12b. The rationale here is contained within the directions. One additional reason for a fishbowl is to give participants more experience in observing group processes.

In the directions, we usually tell them (1) what they are going to do; (2) why they are going to do it; and (3) what to begin doing. Even though 1 and 3 are the same, participants often miss the directions and require a third or fourth repetition.

2:55—3:00
5 minutes

13a. Have the groups switch seats, with the members of the outside group moving inside and discussing for five minutes what they observed about the first group's process. The new outside group will begin taking notes on the new inside group's process.

13b. The critiquing should be noticeably better than it was in the morning.

3:00—3:05
5 minutes

14a. Now the inside group will discuss for five minutes its own process during the jigsaw exercise and may refer to the notes taken, if necessary. The outside group will continue to write down observations of the inside group's process.

3:05—3:10
5 minutes

15a. Have the groups switch seats, with the outside group members moving inside and discussing for five minutes what they observed about the other group's process.

3:10—3:50
40 minutes

16a. In one large group, have all the participants discuss how to implement the jigsaw technique. The teachers will probably want to share descriptions of effective team-building exercises, and will want to discuss problem situations.

16b. Many questions and suggestions will have been stimulated by the day's activities. This discussion gives them time to put everything together. We often discuss specifically what has been working in jigsaw classrooms.

3:50—4:00
10 minutes

17a. Give participants an evaluation sheet on which you encourage them to give feedback for improving the workshop.

17b. It is important for workshop facilitators, as well as for classroom teachers, to invite feedback regularly. Not only is the feedback useful to the facilitator or teacher

but, by increasing the participant
or student's sense of ownership and
control, it quickens interest and
builds morale.

This workshop was designed for teachers who expected to stay until
4:30. We usually end our workshops a half hour early in order to give
teachers a needed rest. Also, this encourages them to give their complete
attention to the end of the workshop.

If there were more time, or if there were another day, this design
could be readily expanded by including such exercises as the Broken
Squares Game or the NASA Exercise, which are described in Appendix
E. Teachers could also work on adapting their curriculum to the jigsaw
technique.

Another useful task, if there is time, is for the teachers to take a few
minutes to form three- or four-person "support groups." These groups
would meet periodically so teachers could share ideas and develop curriculum material. Ideally, each group would consist of same-grade-level
teachers whose schools are near one another.

One of the purposes of this one-day workshop is to whet teachers'
appetites for more. Even with a great deal of support, it has been our
experience that teachers can benefit greatly from further training and
from sharing experiences. After even one brief workshop, however, they
should be able to implement some jigsaw strategies in their classrooms.

A few concluding words on the facilitator. One important role for the
facilitator is to model effective teacher behavior. For example, the facilitator has alternated his short lectures with activities that involve the
participants so that they can learn by doing. In addition, the facilitator
has shown respect for the teachers' own skills by encouraging them to teach
each other. Moreover, rather than merely lecturing, the facilitator often
tied his didactic comments into something the participants had just experienced. He then took that particular example and generalized from it.
For example, after the groups had been observing each other in the morning, he talked about the tendency members of a group might have toward
feeling defensive when they are receiving feedback. He then discussed the
general ways to make feedback more constructive and less threatening.
Finally, throughout the day, he demonstrated sensitivity to the emotional
needs of the participants by providing structures which encouraged them
to experience one another as people and as potential resources.

BROKEN SQUARES GAME

Goals:

(1) To analyze certain aspects of cooperation in solving a group problem.

(2) To sensitize the participants to some of their own behaviors which may contribute toward or obstruct the solving of a group problem.

Group Size:

Any number of groups of six participants each. There will be five participants and an observer/judge. Note: If necessary to balance size of group, the observer/judge role may be eliminated from this activity.

Time Required:

Fifteen to twenty minutes for the exercise and fifteen minutes for discussion.

Materials Utilized:

(1) Chalkboard, chalk, eraser.

(2) Tables that will seat five participants each, or students can sit on the floor.

(3) One set of broken squares for each group of five participants.

Physical Setting:

Tables should be spaced far enough apart so that the various groups cannot observe the activities of other groups.

Process:

The teacher may wish to begin with a discussion of the meaning of co-operation; this should lead to suggestions by the groups of what is essential

---

AUTHOR'S NOTE: The Broken Squares Game was invented by Dr. Alex Bavelas and is reproduced with his permission. See A. Bavelas, Communication patterns in task-oriented groups. *J. Acoustical Society of America,* 1950, *22*, 725-730, and A. Bavelas, The Five Squares Problem: an instructional aid in group cooperation. *Studies in Personnel Psychology*, 1973, *5*, 29-38.

in successful group cooperation. These may be listed on the board, and the teacher may introduce the exercise by indicating that the groups will conduct an experiment to test their suggestions. Basic suggestions which the teacher may want to bring out of the groups are as follows:

(1) Each individual must understand the total problem.

(2) Each individual should understand how he can contribute toward solving the problem.

(3) Each individual should be aware of the potential contributions of other individuals.

(4) There is a need to recognize the problems of other individuals in order to aid them in making their maximum contribution.

Instructions are as follows:

(1) When the preliminary discussion is finished, the teacher asks each group to distribute the envelopes from the prepared packets. The envelopes are to remain unopened until the signal to work is given.

(2) The teacher then reads the instructions to the group, calling for questions, or questioning groups as to their understanding of the instructions. It will be necessary for the teacher to monitor the tables during the exercise to enforce the rules which have been established in the instructions.

(3) When all the groups have completed the task, the teacher will engage the groups in a discussion of the experience. Discussion should focus on feelings more than merely relating experiences and general observations. Observations are solicited from the observer/judge.

DIRECTIONS FOR MAKING A SET OF SQUARES

A set consists of five envelopes containing pieces of cardboard which have been cut into different patterns and which, when properly arranged, will form five squares of equal size. One set should be provided for each group of five persons.

To prepare a set, cut out five cardboard squares of equal size, approximately six by six inches. Place the squares in a row and mark them as below, penciling the letters a, b, c, etc. lightly so that they can later be erased.

The lines should be so drawn that, when cut out, all pieces marked "a" will be of exactly the same size, all pieces marked "c" of the same size,

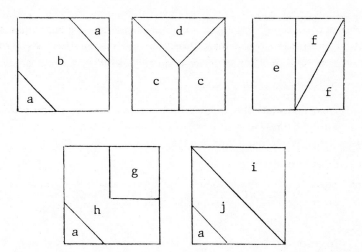

etc. By using multiples of three inches, several combinations will be possible that will enable participants to form one or two squares, but only one combination is possible that will form five six-by-six-inch squares.

After drawing the lines on the six-by-six-inch squares and labeling them with lower-case letters, cut each square as marked into smaller pieces to make the parts of the puzzle.

Mark the five envelopes v, w, x, y, and z. Distribute the cardboard pieces in the five envelopes as follows:

> Envelope v has pieces i, h, e
> Envelope w has pieces a, a, a, c
> Envelope x has pieces a, j
> Envelope y has pieces d, f
> Envelope z has pieces g, b, f, c

Erase the penciled letter from each piece and write, instead, the appropriate envelope letter. This will make it easy to return the pieces to the proper envelope for subsequent use when a group has completed the task.

RULES FOR BROKEN SQUARES GAME

Group Task:

To complete five squares in such a way that each player has a square the same size as the other players. In other words, everybody must end up with the same size square.

Rules:

"The game must be played in complete silence. No talking. You may not point or signal other players with your hands in any way. You may not place a piece in another player's square. You may not take a piece from another player. You *may* give a piece to another player. When you have finished, cover your square with your envelope.

"It's a giving game. Now you'll each get an envelope containing three pieces, but don't open it until I say to. This is a group task and you will have forty minutes to build your squares."

NASA EXERCISE: SEEKING CONSENSUS

Goals:

(1) To compare the results of individual decision-making with the results of group decision-making.

(2) To diagnose the level of development in a task-oriented group.

Group Size:

Between six and twelve participants. Several groups may be directed simultaneously.

Time Required:

Approximately one hour.

Materials Utilized:

(1) Pencils.

(2) Individual work sheets.

(3) Group work sheets.

(4) Answer sheets containing rationale for decisions.

(5) Direction sheets for scoring.

Physical Setting:

Participants should be seated around a square or round table. The dynamics of a group seated at a rectangular table are such that it gives too much control to persons seated at the ends.

AUTHOR'S NOTE: The NASA Exercise was invented by Dr. Jay Hall and is reprinted with his permission.

Process:

(1) Each participant is given a copy of the individual work sheet and told that he has fifteen minutes to complete the exercise.

(2) One group work sheet is handed to each group.

    (a) Individuals *are not* to change any answers on their individual sheets as a result of group discussion.

    (b) A member of the group is to record group consensus on this sheet.

    (c) The participants will have thirty minutes in which to complete the group work sheet.

(3) Each participant is given a copy of the direction sheet for scoring. This phase of the experience should take seven to ten minutes.

    (a) They are to score their individual work sheets.

    (b) They will then give their score to the recorder, who will compute the average of the individual scores.

    (c) The recorder will then score the group work sheet.

(4) The group will compute the average score for individuals with the group score and discuss the implications of the experience. This phase of the experience should take seven to ten minutes.

(5) Results are posted according to the chart below, and the facilitator directs a discussion of the outcomes of consensus-seeking and the experience of negotiating agreement.

	Group 1	Group 2	Group 3
Consensus Score			
Average Score			
Range of Individual Scores			

NASA EXERCISE INDIVIDUAL WORKSHEET

Instructions:

You are a member of a space crew originally scheduled to rendezvous with a mother ship on the lighted surface of the moon. Due to mechanical difficulties, however, your ship was forced to land at a spot some 200 miles from the rendezvous point. During landing, much of the equipment aboard was damaged, and, since survival depends on reaching the mother ship, the most critical items available must be chosen for the 200-mile trip. Below are listed the fifteen items left intact and undamaged after landing. Your task is to rank order them in terms of their importance to your crew in allowing them to reach the rendezvous point. Place the number 1 by the most important item, the number 2 by the second most important, and so on, through number 15, the least important. *You have fifteen minutes to complete this phase of the exercise.*

_____ Box of matches

_____ Food concentrate

_____ 50 feet of nylon rope

_____ Parachute silk

_____ Portable heating unit

_____ Two .45 calibre pistols

_____ One case dehydrated Pet milk

_____ Two 100-lb. tanks of oxygen

_____ Stellar map (of the moon's constellation)

_____ Life raft

_____ Magnetic compass

_____ 5 gallons of water

_____ Signal flares

_____ First-aid kit containing injection needles

_____ Solar-powered FM receiver-transmitter

NASA EXERCISE GROUP WORKSHEET

Instructions:

This is an exercise in group decision-making. Your group is to employ the method of *Group Consensus* in reaching its decision. This means that the prediction for each of the fifteen survival items *must* be agreed upon by each group member before it becomes a part of the group decision. Consensus is difficult to reach. Therefore, not every ranking will meet with everyone's complete *approval.* Try, as a group, to make each ranking one with which *all* group members can at least partially agree. Here are some guides to use in reaching consensus:

(1) Avoid arguing for your own individual judgments. Approach the task on the basis of logic.

(2) Avoid changing your mind only in order to reach agreement and avoid conflict. Support only solutions with which you are able to agree somewhat, at least.

(3) Avoid "conflict-reducing" techniques such as majority vote, averaging, or trading in reaching your decision.

(4) View differences of opinion as helpful rather than as a hindrance in decision-making.

_____ Box of matches

_____ Food concentrate

_____ 50 feet of nylon rope

_____ Parachute silk

_____ Portable heating unit

_____ Two .45 calibre pistols

_____ One case dehydrated Pet milk

_____ Two 100-lb. tanks of oxygen

_____ Stellar map (of moon's constellation)

_____ Life raft

_____ Magnetic compass

_____ 5 gallons of water

_____ Signal flares

_____ First-aid kit containing injection needles

_____ Solar-powered FM receiver-transmitter

NASA EXERCISE ANSWER SHEET

Rationale:	Correct Number:	
No oxygen	15	Box of matches
Can live for some time without food	4	Food concentrate
For travel over rough terrain	6	50 feet of nylon rope
Carrying	8	Parachute silk
Lighted side of moon is hot	13	Portable heating unit
Some use for propulsion	11	Two .45 calibre pistols
Needs H_2O to work	12	One case dehydrated Pet milk
No air on moon	1	Two 100-lb. tanks of oxygen
Needed for navigation	3	Stellar map (of moon's constellation)
Some value for shelter or carrying	9	Life raft
Moon's magnetic field is different from earth's	14	Magnetic Compass
You can't live long without this	2	5 gallons of water
No oxygen	10	Signal flares
First-aid kit might be needed but needles are useless	7	First-aid kit containing injection needles
Communication	5	Solar-powered FM receiver-transmitter

NASA EXERCISE DIRECTION SHEET FOR SCORING

The group recorder will assume the responsibility for directing the scoring. Individuals will:

(1) Score the net difference between their answers and correct answers. For example, if the answer was 9, and the correct answer was 12, the net difference is 3. Three becomes the score for that particular item.

(2) Total these scores for an individual score.

(3) Next, total all individual scores and divide by the number of participants to arrive at an average individual score.

(4) Score the net difference between group worksheet answers and the correct answers.

(5) Total these scores for a group score.

(6) Compare the average individual score with the group score.

Ratings:

0—20	Excellent
20—30	Good
30—40	Average
40—50	Fair
over 50	Poor

References

Aronson, E., N. Blaney, J. Sikes, C. Stephan, and M. Snapp. "Busing and racial tension: The jigsaw route to learning and liking," *Psychology Today* 8, (1975): pp. 43-59.

Aronson, E., N. Blaney, and C. Stephan. Cooperation in the classroom: The jigsaw puzzle model. Paper presented at the meetings of the American Psychological Association, September 1975.

Blaney, N. T., C. Stephan, D. Rosenfield, E. Aronson, and J. Sikes. "Interdependence in the classroom: A field study," *Journal of Educational Psychology* 69, (1977): pp. 121-128.

Bridgeman, D. L. The influence of cooperative, interdependent learning on role taking and moral reasoning: A theoretical and empirical field study with fifth-grade students. Unpublished doctoral dissertation, University of California, Santa Cruz, 1977.

Brookover, W. B., A. Patterson, and S. Thomas. "Self-concept of ability and school achievement," *Sociology of Education* 37, (1964): pp. 271-278.

Chandler, M. J. "Egocentrism and antisocial behavior: The assessment and training of social perspective-taking skills," *Developmental Psychology* 9, (1973): pp. 326-332.

Cloward, R. "Studies in tutoring," *Journal of Experimental Education* 36, (1967): pp. 14-25.

Coleman, J. S. *Equality of Educational Opportunity*. U.S. Dept. of Health, Education, and Welfare, Washington, D.C., 1966.

Courtis, S., E. McSwain, and N. Morrison. *Teachers and Cooperation*. Washington, D.C.: National Education Association, 1937.

Covington, M. V. and R. G. Beery. *Self-worth and School Learning*. New York: Holt, Rinehart, and Winston, 1976.

Deutsch, M. "A theory of cooperation and competition." *Human Relations* 2, (1949): pp. 129-152.

DeVries, D. L. Teams-games-tournament: Five years of research. Paper presented at the annual meeting of the American Psychological Association, September 1977.

Franks, D. D. and J. Marolla. "Efficacious action and social approval as interacting dimensions of self-esteem: A tentative formulation through construct validation," *Sociometry* 39, (1976): pp. 324-341.

Garibaldi, A. Cooperation, competition, individualization, and black students' problem solving and attitudes. Paper presented at the annual meeting of the American Psychological Association, September 1977.

Geffner, R. A. The effects of interdependent learning on self-esteem, inter-ethnic relations, and intra-ethnic attitudes of elementary school children: A field experiment. Unpublished doctoral dissertation, University of California, Santa Cruz, 1978.

Gerard, H. and N. Miller. *School Desegregation*. New York: Plenum Press, 1975.

Haines, D. B. and W. J. McKeachie. "Cooperative versus competitive discussion methods in teaching introductory psychology," *Journal of Educational Psychology* 58, (1967): pp. 386-390.

Heider, F. *The Psychology of Interpersonal Relations.* New York: John Wiley, 1958.

Holt, J. *How Children Learn.* New York: Dell, 1967.

Johnson, D. and R. Johnson. *Learning Together and Alone.* Englewood Cliffs, N.J.: Prentice-Hall, 1975.

Johnson, D. W. and R. T. Johnson. Cooperation, competition, and individualization and interracial, intersexual, and interability attitudes. Paper presented at the annual meeting of the American Psychological Association, September 1977.

Johnson, D., R. Johnson, and R. Scott. "The effects of cooperative and individualized instruction on student attitudes and achievement," *Journal of Social Psychology*, 1978, in press.

Jones, E. E. and K. E. Davis. "From acts to dispositions," in L. Berkowitz (ed.), *Advances in Experimental Social Psychology,* Volume 2. New York: Academic Press, 1965.

Kagan, S. and M. C. Madsen. "Cooperation and competition of Mexican, Mexican-American, and Anglo-American children of two ages under four instructional sets," *Developmental Psychology* 5, (1971): pp. 32-39.

Lippitt, P., J. Eiseman, and R. Lippitt. *Cross-age Helping Program: Orientation, Training, and Related Materials.* Ann Arbor: University of Michigan, Center for Research on Utilization of Scientific Knowledge, Institute for Social Research, 1969.

Lippitt, P. and J. Lohman. "Cross-age relationships—an educational resource," *Children* 12, (1965): pp. 113-117.

Lucker, G. W., D. Rosenfield, J. Sikes, and E. Aronson. "Performance in the interdependent classroom: A field study," *American Educational Research Review* 13, (1977): pp. 115-123.

Madsen, M. C. "Cooperative and competitive motivation of children in three Mexican subcultures," *Psychological Reports* 20, (1967): pp. 1307-1320.

——— "Developmental and cross-cultural differences in cooperative and competitive behavior of young children," *Journal of Cross-Cultural Psychology* 2, (1971): pp. 365-371.

——— and A. Shapira. "Cooperative and competitive behavior of urban Afro-American, Anglo-American, Mexican-American, and Mexican village children," *Developmental Psychology* 3, (1970): pp. 16-20.

Nelson, L. L. and S. Kagan. "Competition: The star-spangled scramble," *Psychology Today* 6, (September 1972): p. 53.

Phillips, B. N. and L. A. D'Amico. "Effects of cooperation and competition on the cohesiveness of small face-to-face groups," *Journal of Educational Psychology* 47, (1956): pp. 65-70.

Postman, N. and C. Weingartner. *Teaching as a Subversive Activity.* New York: Delta, 1969.

Purkey, W. W. *Self-Concept and School Achievement.* Englewood Cliffs, N.J.: Prentice-Hall, 1970.

Slavin, J. E. Student teams and peer tutoring. Paper presented at the annual meeting of the American Psychological Association, September 1977.

Slavin, R. Student team-learning techniques: Narrowing the gap between the races. 1977. Report No. 228, Center for Social Organization of Schools, Johns Hopkins University, Baltimore, Md.

Stendler, C., D. Damrin, and A. C. Haines. "Studies in cooperation and competition: 1. The effects of working for group and individual rewards on the social climate of children's groups," *Journal of Genetic Psychology* 79, (1951): pp. 173-197.

Stephan, C., J. C. Kennedy, and E. Aronson. "The effects of friendship and outcome on task attribution," *Sociometry* 40, (1977): pp. 107-111.

Stephan, W. "School desegregation: An evaluation of predictions made in Brown v. the Board of Education," *Psychological Bulletin,* 1978, in press.

Weigel, R. H., P. L. Wiser, and S. W. Cook. "The impact of cooperative learning experiences on cross-ethnic relations and attitudes," *Journal of Social Issues* 31, (1975): pp. 219-244.

About the Authors

ELLIOT ARONSON is Professor of Psychology at the University of California at Santa Cruz. He received his B.A. from Brandeis in 1954, his M.A. from Wesleyan in 1956 and his Ph.D. in Psychology from Stanford in 1959. Dr. Aronson has taught at Harvard, the University of Texas, and the University of Minnesota. His publications include over sixty articles in scholarly journals and ten books including the monumental *Handbook of Social Psychology* (with Gardner Lindzey in 1968), *The Social Animal* (1972), and *Methods of Research in Social Psychology* (1976). He was awarded the Sociopsychological Prize for Creative Research in 1970 by the American Association for the Advancement of Science; in 1973, the American Psychological Association presented him with the National Media Award for his book, *The Social Animal.* In 1974, the Texas Classroom Teachers Association presented him with its Human Relations Award for his work related to the contents of the present volume. Dr. Aronson has been married for twenty-three years and has four children, who went through the public schools in various cities across the country. He has been twice a Fellow at the Center for Advanced Study in the Behavioral Sciences.

NANCY BLANEY is a social psychologist with a background in community psychology and communication. She received her Ph.D. in 1974 from the University of Texas at Austin and completed a two-year training program at NTL in Bethel, Maine, focusing upon group leader training, organization and community development, and innovative educational approaches. Her interests center upon using social psychology as a tool for studying social issues, such as integration, in the social context in which they occur. For the past four years, she was Assistant Professor in the School of Communication at the University of Texas at Austin. She now resides in Coral Gables, Florida, where she is pursuing research in the psychosocial factors in disease etiology and how such risk factors may be modified in social settings.

COOKIE STEPHAN received her Ph.D. from the Laboratory for Research in Social Relations in the Department of Psychology at the University of Minnesota. She is now an Assistant Professor in the Department of Sociology at the University of Texas at Austin. Dr. Stephan is a social psychologist with research interests in cooperation/competition, attribution theory, physical attractiveness, as well as sex roles, occupational aspirations, and jury decisions. She has contributed field and laboratory research to psychology and sociology journals in the United States and Europe. Dr. Stephan is coauthor of *Social Problems and Human Responses,* Dorsey, 1978.

JEV SIKES grew up in Boulder, Colorado, where he learned to love the wilderness. After getting his B.A. in English from Carleton College, he attended Harvard Divinity School for a year on a Rockefeller Fellowship. He then obtained his Ph.D. in Counseling Psychology at the University of Texas in Austin, and is currently an Associate Professor of Psychology at Southwest Texas State. He has consulted with educational and business organizations around the country, particularly with respect to interpersonal communication problems, and along with his wife Sydnor, has owned and directed a human relations oriented, survival training, backpacking camp in Colorado. He plays tennis daily, and is still an avid skier and hiker.

MATTHEW SNAPP has a strong background in both education and psychology. He received his B.A. from Wagner College in New York, his M.A. from Brigham Young University in Utah, and his Ph.D. from the University of Texas at Austin. He has been a classroom teacher, a school counselor, a school psychologist, and is currently Director of the Student Development Department for the Austin Public Schools. He has consulted with many groups including teachers, counselors, psychologists, and administrators, and his assistance has been sought by such diverse groups as a corrections facility for juvenile offenders and dentists and their staffs. In addition to these many activities he has an appointment as Adjunct Assistant Professor and is a member of the graduate faculty in the Department of Educational Psychology at the University of Texas. His interest in cooperative educational techniques grew out of his experiences with desegregating schools.